Winning the
TALENT
SHIFT

Winning the
TALENT
SHIFT

Three Steps to Unleashing the New High Performance Workplace

BERTA ALDRICH

WILEY

Published by John Wiley & Sons, Inc., Hoboken, New Jersey.

Published simultaneously in Canada.

For general information on our other products and services or for technical support, please contact our Customer Care Department within the United States at (800) 762–2974, outside the United States at (317) 572–3993, or fax (317) 572–4002.

Wiley publishes in a variety of print and electronic formats and by print-on-demand. Some material included with standard print versions of this book may not be included in e-books or in print-on-demand. If this book refers to media such as a CD or DVD that is not included in the version you purchased, you may download this material at http://booksupport.wiley.com. For more information about Wiley products, visit www.wiley.com.

Library of Congress Cataloging-in-Publication Data is available:

ISBN 9781119768715 (Hardcover)
ISBN 9781119768517 (ePDF)
ISBN 9781119768722 (ePub)

Cover Design: Wiley

Printed in the United States of America.

SKY10021534_093020

Dedicated to
Mike, Aaron & Lauren

For
Women, high performers and true leaders everywhere

Contents

Foreword

When I was asked to take the helm at Nutrisystem as CEO, the first two things I tackled, in what would eventually be described as a remarkable corporate turnaround, were improving the culture and ensuring that the right people were in the right seats. Diverse perspectives and voices were critical to me as we set forth a vision and strategy and rolled up our sleeves for the hard work necessary to transform the company.

Without a doubt, my biggest success factor as CEO was assembling my executive team and the deliberate way in which we worked together. The team consisted of several superstars I inherited, newcomers I brought in from my network, a diverse mix of accomplished men and women, and several individuals who had left the company years before and whom I was able to entice back. We were a team that was aligned in both mission and passion, plus we valued the uniqueness of thought and debate that each of us brought to the conversation. We encouraged our teams to challenge underlying assumptions and the status quo. We asked people to step out of their comfort zone, we stayed open to a new way of doing things, and we empowered everyone throughout the organization to share his or her voice.

We operated with candor, avoided politics, set high standards for integrity and performance, and held people accountable. Alignment with our cultural values was something we talked about extensively, both internally and with candidates, as we morphed from looking for those who would be a good cultural fit to those who could culturally enhance us.

In short, selecting the right people for your leadership roles and embracing diversity is critical for every organization. I found it equally important to establish accountability in upholding a culture that promotes the right behavior and doesn't turn a blind eye to cultural erosion. As a board member and as an executive, these are the things that we have to get right, as we've seen way too many companies become *Wall Street Journal* headlines for failing to do so.

That is why this book is so important and worth a read. There are barriers in today's workplace and this book candidly illuminates them. As executives, we cannot ignore that they happen. It's our role to create environments in which our people can succeed – for themselves, for our companies, and for our shareholders. It's time for a shift. . . .

Dawn Zier

August 2020

Acknowledgments

It's funny how life sets you on one path and you end up somewhere else. In looking back, this book came to fruition because of the generosity, encouragement, and investment of time of family, friends, and acquaintances.

I originally set out to fulfill a dream of writing a book for our daughter, Lauren, to give to her upon her college graduation. She was attending college to pursue a marketing degree and I, as a mom and as someone who had a lifelong career in business, wanted to give her the gift that no one else could – my workplace and life wisdom. Even more, I wanted to pass along to her the collective wisdom of not only my own experiences, but those of the thousands I had mentored, taught, or helped along their journey.

Through a series of events, it became clear that the contents of the book could help more people, and *Winning the Talent Shift* was born. I am a true believer that no one can go through this life alone and it takes people who are willing to help and encourage others to bring your vision, passion, and purpose to life.

To my family: Mike, Aaron, and Lauren. Mike, my best friend and partner in life, the one who makes me laugh and challenges me intellectually: this would not have happened without supporting my extra time outside the formal workplace. Thank you for trusting in me, for your undying support, and for going on this crazy journey together. Aaron, for your unapologetic approach to doing what you were meant to do in life and pursuing it; for your integrity, brilliance, and sense of duty to others, including this great country. You exhibit all that is right, ethically, morally, and in faith, and you stand by your core beliefs with passion. You inspire me each and every day. And to Lauren, thank you for agreeing to share your very personal gift with the goal of wanting anyone who is talented, smart, and driven to be able to achieve their dream, as you will also achieve yours. You are my inspiration and drive to make the workplace a better place for incredible talent like you. May you always carry the confidence, grace, and grit you exhibit today forward into the workplace and life.

To my mom, for being the best, first great leader I experienced in my life. Seven children, a full-time job, countless volunteer activities, and president of a nonprofit to help special ability people, you did it all and with the grace and determination of a warrior. You allowed each one of us to be the best of who we were, leveraging our innate talents to find what truly made us happy in life and to pursue it. You are amazing and have set the bar so high that I can only strive to achieve. Your undying support, resilience, belief in all good with one eye open to those who are not, your strong faith, and your strength and wisdom have carried me through life and encouraged me to achieve everything I was meant to be – and do. I thank God for you every day.

To Vanessa, for your relentless support, positivity, and encouragement and believing that this book would come to fruition and help others. To Val, who inspires me through faith every minute of every day (I love you more), and to Chuck, Dan, and Pat, for being those good guys in life. To Bill and Sandy, for your support and for giving me one of the greatest gifts: your son. I love you all dearly.

To my friends and colleagues who encouraged me to pursue writing for the masses and provided feedback and candid insights that helped set the direction for this book. Rachel and Marie, thank you for sharing your wisdom and learnings from your own success that lighted my path. Julie, Paula, Joyce, Jenn, Melissa, Jennifer, Bill,

Ed, Kevin, Jennifer, Christine, Tara, Sterling, and Diana for your insight, encouragement, and support. You are my village.

To the PAG family, specifically Pat and John, who not only supported the message of this book, but encouraged getting its content to the masses. Thank you for creating a high-performance workplace and your continued belief that we can all make a difference in our industry and in our world. To my peers Jim, James, and Jim, who have been equally supportive, encouraging, and willing to take this ride together.

To the Wiley family, Bill, Purvi, and Samantha. Thank you for believing in this message and lending your expertise, vision, and talent to this book. The end result was made better because of you.

I'm also eternally grateful for my colleagues who have taught me so much, who challenged me, stood with me, and were willing to do what is right, even when those around us did not. I could never thank you all, but a few who were especially inspiring for the writing of this book include Dar, who was a true trailblazer and taught me that women can be smart, driven, educated, great leaders, and make a positive impact. Dan, who is hands down the best leader I've ever met: it is an honor to call you my friend. I've learned so much from you throughout my career. You are the perfect combination of brilliance, drive, and humility. Bert, who exhibited what true loyalty, mentorship, and sponsorship was as a leader. Dave D., whose support came at a critical point in my career and tipping point as a mother. Dave W., who gave me opportunities to spread my wings throughout my career. Tom, who has always believed in my talent and impact, and gave me opportunities I could only have dreamed of. Kevin, for inviting me to be part of something bigger than ourselves. Dawn, for being part of your amazing Go Red team. Watching you lead was life changing. You are a true leader. Shannon, who was a perfect example of supporting the greater mission without caring who received the credit. Karin, for being a true leader during a critical meeting that changed the trajectory of my life's purpose, and 1,000-plus other lives across the globe.

To Liz, for your friendship and life's work to create great leaders in the city of Philadelphia and beyond.

To those who have gone before *Winning the Talent Shift*, especially Joanna Barsh and Sheryl Sandberg, your groundbreaking research and books opened the door for this conversation.

To Shawn and Ed: Without you this book would not have been possible. Ed, your grace, talent, and faith became a critical component of carefully communicating this important message. Thank you for your insight, lending your talent, and incredibly strong words of wisdom and faith throughout the process.

Finally, to all of the incredible mentors, mentees, sponsors, Remarkable Women and Men, and other great leaders I've encountered over the years, thank you for being part of my life's work. I hope this book pays forward the many insights and wisdom you have provided over the years.

In the end, our greatest successes come from our willingness to help others. Thank you to all who have been part of this amazing journey.

–Berta

Winning the
TALENT
SHIFT

PART

I

The Reality–
Why We Need
a Shift

1

What We're Missing

"Conformity is the jailer of freedom and the enemy of growth."
— John F. Kennedy

Leadership is the highest honor in the business world.

High-performing leaders are the prisms that expand the variety of talents and expertly inspire the greatest possible impact from each person on their teams. They invest in them, develop them, and help them achieve more than they imagined. They ignite a spark that helps them create something bigger than themselves. True leaders have accepted a vitally important mission.

Great leaders are inspiring visionaries. They develop and promote high performers who have a passion for delivering great results with integrity, teamwork, and grit. They give credit where credit is due and pay their success forward. Their greatest accomplishments are their teams, and it's pure joy to stand back and watch them excel. If leadership is the highest honor in the business world, then leading a team to high performance where everyone contributes their best is the Holy Grail that every great leader should aspire to achieve.

★★★★★

The workplace is changing at an accelerated pace. Over the past 30 years, companies have been required to adapt to global competition, leaps in technology, more highly educated workers, emerging consumers, and innovations that have created unrestricted business opportunities. At the same time, more women and highly educated talent are entering the workplace than ever before, introducing new ways of thinking, leading, inspiring, and engaging to meet these new demands. The unmanaged sea change has created devastating effects on the workplace, placing women and this new high-performing talent squarely in the center of the war. These key groups are vulnerable, unprotected, and at risk because today's boards and executives are using a bottom-up, groundswell marketing strategy to manage the change, failing to lead their companies through one of the greatest transformations in business history. This has left companies at substantial risk for future lawsuits, failed brands, and underperforming teams, potentially costing shareholders billions of dollars each year. The overwhelming research and anecdotal evidence today suggest that the majority of companies are failing to tap into the exceptional talent already present within their walls. This is especially true for women, but also affects men. Pointing fingers at men has only exacerbated the separation of genders into silos of talent.

The answer is not pitting men and women against each other or continuing to encourage cultures where only the strong survive. For companies to adapt to the current market opportunities and to create a high-performing workplace that leverages the variety of talents already available, the company of the future must be equipped with the tools to integrate, inspire, and empower their teams.

Today's workplace and current leaders have not been adequately prepared for the influx of different talents, genders, and beliefs. Training on diversity and encouraging women to "Lean In" is only exacerbating the worst of situations and has resulted in overly competitive, "win at any cost" HR systems that tend to inaccurately identify and promote leaders unprepared to maximize the talent of these new, diverse teams.

Companies can shift away from their destructive practices, and instead maximize their teams, gain a competitive advantage in their industries, and achieve cultures in which inspired and engaged teams and leaders produce great results. Helping leaders identify why they're failing to foster high-performing teams and giving them simple steps that virtually assure high performance across their companies is my personal mission and the focus of this book.

First, a personal story to highlight the high stakes and to share a path toward a solution.

★★★★★

My team and I were still elated after winning an industry award the prior month (our fourth) for our leadership in rebranding and remarketing our firm. By all measures, we were a high-performing team, delivering great work, supporting each other, supporting our fellow colleagues, and delivering highly acclaimed, world-renowned results. As a leader, it didn't get any better than this. The team was engaged and empowered and so was I. By all external measures, I was a high-performing leader, leading a high-performing team.

A few weeks later, my job was eliminated. No explanation. No warning.

My mind was reeling. I had never been out of a job before. I had worked countless hours each week, at a job I loved, with a team I loved, producing great results for the organization. Why now? I had so many questions.

After a year filled with a lot of prayer and soul searching, it all became clear, but I'll share that lesson with you later.

Over the course of my one-year noncompete, I continued to mentor men and women in the workplace – most of whom were high performers. Mentoring others from outside the workplace for the first time in my career gave me new insight and a fresh perspective. I found myself responding to their challenges by sharing similar experiences of navigating the pitfalls of corporate life and noticed that women and men have the same challenges. Each conflict we discussed involved a high performer and an overly aggressive manager, typically a higher-level executive or a peer on a quest for more power.

When I was immersed in the workplace, I would have encouraged my mentees to "Lean In" to their challenges and then provide solutions based on the wisdom found on those pages and in other books that advise top performers to simply play within the sandbox they are given. **With the clarity of an outside perspective, my mentoring shifted to questioning why those who are targeted and undermined stay at companies that mistreat them. I wanted to empower my mentees to create change and to stand up for themselves, but they couldn't. These bullies were powerful and sat in some of the highest positions in their organizations.** Perhaps it took so much time to notice this bullying behavior at the highest levels of the corporate world because, regardless of your level in the workplace, it's the norm – an accepted cultural behavior regarded as part of the "game." From the outside, it simply mirrors a fifth grader bullying a first grader on an elementary school playground.

Helping my mentees "Lean In" to conflict with a superior most likely meant "Leaning In" to a 3:00 p.m. meeting with HR on a Friday. They lacked the influence to change the rules. I noticed that high performers, particularly high-potential leaders and women in general, appeared to be targeted 100% of the time. Women tended to have less insight into why their superiors were targeting them, which required more conversation around *why* they were marginalized, overlooked, bullied, or abused. Each woman had a hard time processing the reality that, in most cases, it wasn't their fault. The men, to their credit, had a much more innate sense of how to move forward, mostly by hitting the issue head-on. Unfortunately, that approach backfired for women.

After experiencing several of the same conversations, a recurring problem emerged. Despite a desire to hire highly qualified men and women, most organizations are not designed to promote, support, or identify high performers – especially among women. Dropping talented women into corporate environments, traditionally dominated by men, without a plan for high-performance, mixed-gender teams, has resulted in defensiveness and conflict, often derailing the most competent women and mitigating their value. Men have been held back and derailed by this conflict in the workplace as well, but, fortunately, are more likely to have the capacity to endure it. Women are often blindsided by such conflicts and end up blaming themselves. This unmanaged conflict has allowed the wrong leaders to find opportunity in the chaos, mastering the art of politics and maneuvering their way into once-coveted leadership positions. These "old world" leaders are now in higher positions, seeking to defend their turf and overpower any perceived competitors, failing to effectively lead the transformation as a result.

During one pivotal mentoring session, an up-and-coming female leader shared how she had been derailed by a senior manager one level above her. She felt that it was common knowledge within the organization that the senior manager had risen to the executive ranks because she knew how to navigate and eliminate her competition. This executive bullied and discredited anyone in her path. I had unfortunately crossed paths with this executive as well, and ultimately survived, but not without earning a few battle scars to prove it. I survived out of sheer grit and tenacity, never willing to give up.

I had just finished this mentoring conversation when our daughter, Lauren, came home from high school and shared how she had heard of a girl being bullied. The girl targeted by the bullies was a good person who had done nothing to provoke the incident, and my daughter had reached out to her in support. Lauren was captain of the cheer team, a role that could be used for good in these types of situations, and she didn't disappoint. It wasn't the first time she would help someone being bullied, and I suspect it won't be the last. I was so proud of this young woman and the leader she had become, and then my mind drifted to imagining her in the workplace. How was she, and all of her smart, talented friends, going to survive? The work-place is full of bullies. How would she effectively stand up to a bully in the workplace who could eliminate her position or undermine her career? She was showing signs of being a great leader, but would she encounter the same dysfunction I did? The high performers I continue to mentor, and the over 1,000 men and women I've men-tored or instructed over the years, all experienced similar barriers that kept them from performing at their best.

The workplace is not ready for my daughter, her generation, or even *this* current generation of top performers. Something needed to change. As one of my mentors once told me, the answer lies in the root cause. So I set out on a journey to help my daughter, her friends, the high performers I had mentored, and those I have never met. Here is the irony in what I found:

Today's companies are in a war for talent, seeking to hire women and high performers who provide exponential perfor-mance impact in today's hypercompetitive global marketplace. Unfortunately, most executives and HR departments don't realize that many of the talented individuals who can maximize high performance in organizations – women, top performers, and inspiring leaders – are under siege in corporate America. The statistics for workplace bullying alone are staggering, with their direct or indirect impact extending to nearly 75% of the workplace. Turnover among female employees at some companies is as high as 27%, more than double the rate of 11% among men, even though record numbers of women are graduating from college and entering the workforce.[1] To date, the solution offered to

---

[1]Lam, Bouree, "Why Women Shouldn't Have to Act Like Dudes at Work," *The Atlantic*, July 27, 2015, https://www.theatlantic.com/

tormented and derailed high performers and women is little more than encouragement to stay in a corporate game that is often rigged by the design of toxic leaders who aim to eliminate or sabotage the high performers who threaten their turf. The result? Companies are failing the very employees they are responsible to lead, losing the war for talent, compromising their bottom line, and degrading their brands.

A majority of companies today have failed to identify the reason for this war for talent in their organization and are weaker because of it. The root cause? The unidentified war *on* talent is inhibiting companies who want to win the war *for* talent. There is a better way.

War for Talent	Internal Challenge for Companies
Competing to recruit the top talent available.	Retaining top talent despite internal bullying, derailing by managers, and leadership that lacks accountability.
A shift to high performance seeks the right kind of talent and makes a company attractive to potential hires on the job market.	A shift to high performance helps retain top talent by empowering and promoting the best leaders and employees.

If today's boards and C-suite leaders know that adding more women to the workplace, placing great leaders in key positions, and developing and promoting high performers are the three keys to designing a high-performance workplace, why are they allowing the undermining of these groups? After analyzing over 30 years of mentoring sessions with women and men, women in leadership programs that spanned the globe, and my own quest to become a high-performing leader, I found something both concerning and

business/archive/2015/07/women-work-gender-equality-workplace/399503/.

sobering: today's companies are not designed for high performance. In fact, they suppress and eliminate the true high performers and the most effective gender-balanced teams that have proved in multiple studies to inspire creativity, increase profits, and move companies to industry leadership. Today's bottom-up, groundswell strategy of adding more women and talent to the workplace is not working and has left many highly qualified women and men to find their own way through toxic and sometimes illegal barriers in the workplace.

It's time for a new approach that places the responsibility for creating gender-balanced, high-performing organizations squarely in the hands of the very individuals who are in positions of power and can make the change happen: the boards, executives, and leaders within organizations. We should no longer ask women, true leaders, and high performers to play a game they cannot win or be responsible for changing the rules of the game. Instead, they are the reason to *change* the game. The barriers they experience each and every day have reached staggering and epidemic proportions:

- 75% of women have reported abuse in the workplace, and 70% of those have been retaliated against. Women can be exceptional leaders, yet only 1 in 5 women holds a C-suite role.
- High performers produce 200–500% more than an average employee, yet are targeted by imposter leaders almost 100% of the time, and are more likely than an average performer to leave organizations.
- According to Gallup, great leadership is the number-one determinant of a company's success, but less than 25% of leaders today are considered great. How are companies developing the other 75% of their leaders?
- Gallup also found that a staggering 35% of managers are actively engaged with their work. While 51% are simply not engaged with their work, an additional 14% are completely checked out, actively disengaged from their responsibilities.[2]

---

[2]Adkins, Amy, "Only 35% of US Managers Are Engaged in Their Jobs," *Gallup*, April 2, 2015, https://www.gallup.com/workplace/236552/managers-engaged-jobs.aspx.

THE "CASCADE EFFECT" ON EMPLOYEE ENGAGEMENT

Leaders' engagement directly affects managers' engagement — and manager engagement, in turn, directly influences employee engagement. Managers who are directly supervised by highly engaged leadership teams are 39% more likely to be engaged than managers who are supervised by actively disengaged leadership teams. The link between engaged managers and engaged employees is even more powerful — employees who are supervised by highly engaged managers are 59% more likely to be engaged than those supervised by actively disengaged managers.

MANAGERS WHO WORK FOR ENGAGED LEADERS ARE 39% MORE LIKELY TO BE ENGAGED

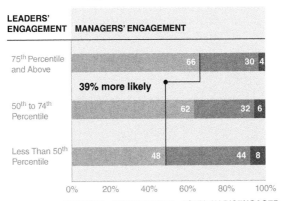

EMPLOYEES WHO WORK FOR ENGAGED MANAGERS ARE 59% MORE LIKELY TO BE ENRAGED

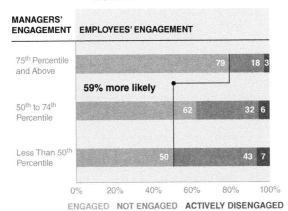

GALLUP'

It's time to show boards, executives, women, and high performers how to create a high-performing workplace by recognizing the barriers, replacing them with more effectual attributes, and redesigning their workplace to create the potential for sustainable growth and industry leadership for years to come.

The good news: the boards and leaders of any company can use this step-by-step guide to attract and to retain top talent in the market, taking their innovation and profits to new heights. I'll show you the key that will unlock the high-performance potential of all employees so that companies can capitalize on new business opportunities and win their industry's war for talent.

Without a plan for high performance in place, these organizations will fail to reach new heights or to maximize their talent. Perhaps companies fail to achieve high performance because (1) they refuse to make the necessary changes or (2) they simply don't know how to effectively integrate high performers and women into their teams and to remove the barriers they face. My bet is on option two.

In fact, most CEOs and C-suite leaders strive to cultivate a high-performing organization, but they are mired in antiquated methods and infrastructures that prohibit them from reaching their own full potential. Organizations are hindered by individuals who are willing to undermine colleagues for the sake of advancing their own careers. Unfortunately, these self-serving individuals are good at playing the game, using a company's culture to their own advantage, at the expense of high performers and shareholders. Today's HR typically chalks these up as "personality conflicts," never truly addressing the underlying and pervasive issue.

How do talented, high-performing individuals flourish and make an impact in this kind of workplace?

In order for highly talented women and men to succeed, companies must make a shift toward a high-performance system, making it possible for the *right* individuals to flourish and enabling teams to function at peak capacity. The power, influence, and responsibility for making this shift rests squarely on the board and current executive leaders. Here is the hard truth that competitive companies of the future need to face:

> It's time for leaders to stop expecting change to come from the bottom of the organization.

Today's workplace is not designed for high performers to succeed, even if HR successfully recruits a talented and diverse workforce. Individuals who are primarily driven to achieve a title, rather than to produce excellent work, can navigate their way to management or leadership positions (let's call them imposters) by bullying their peers and blocking high performers, especially women, from advancing or achieving success. Imposters are primarily driven by their own personal and professional achievements, resorting to aggressive bullying tactics to defend their turf. Today's true high performers (those who are highly ethical and have integrity, intellect, drive, and great leadership traits while also competing externally) make it because of sheer grit and determination. Most of them do not.

If the imposters are the ones making it to the top and are not the true high performers, then workplaces today are not maximizing the potential of the true top performers and women today in leadership positions. What would it take for a company to make this shift to a culture and infrastructure system that allows high performers to succeed and for gender balance to become the norm while minimizing the harm caused by imposters? If companies want to retain excellent employees, to maximize profits, and to ensure that only the best performers advance to key leadership roles, including the C-suite, then what is the one thing that will make the shift possible?

It's time for leaders to stop expecting change to come from the bottom of the organization.

To make change happen, companies must adopt a *top-down approach*. The responsibility for making a shift to high performance rests solely on the current board and C-suite's shoulders, the same people who are responsible for creating the high-performing organization. In defining the roles and responsibilities involved in making this shift, we need to get a handle on the key players who can make this vitally important change happen.

Roles for Leaders at the Top to Make the Shift

Board	Executive Team
Strategic direction	Execute strategic direction
High-level goals	Responsible for profits and shareholder value
Hire CEO	Awareness of the competition
Hire key C-suite positions	Manage the firm's resources
Guidance and accountability	Make decisions on talent

Boards set the strategic direction for the organization. They are typically comprised of high-level leaders from a variety of industries who are paid to provide oversight and diversity of thought and experiences. Boards establish talent and succession planning, set the business strategy, and ensure appropriate capital deployment. They recruit the CEO and are typically involved in the hiring of key positions, including the C-suite, those corporate officers, whose titles begin with C (e.g., CFO, COO, CIO, or CTO). They are the guiding force of the organization. Accountability for the success of the company starts with them.

The executive leadership team executes the strategic direction. C-suite executives have highly impactful and coveted positions in their organizations. They are responsible for their company's profitability and are ultimately accountable for shareholder value. They lead other executives internally while keeping a watchful eye on the competition and ensure that their company goals and ultimate strategy are being fully executed. They manage the firm's resources and make decisions on talent management. These leaders are typically compensated well for their role in the organization. Great leaders are visionary, are ethical, maximize resources (both dollars and talent), are fair, create inspired teams, and are strategic.

The number-one problem with today's organizations is this: too many people in leadership positions are imposters who disenfranchise the true high performers, mitigate the organization's existing talent, and undermine anyone perceived as a threat.

To make a fundamental shift to high performance, the board needs to establish the company's vision, goals, and direction, while the executive leadership needs to be held accountable to make the shift happen. That is how it works with every other goal within an organization, and a goal around high performance that maximizes a company's most important asset should be no different.

If boards and leadership want to achieve high performance, outpace their competition, and lead their respective industries, the one thing that I uncovered (and, remarkably, experienced) is the need to start with an intentional *integration* of high-performing, gender-balanced talent in an organization's leadership. Specifically, teams comprised of a balance of men and women are tomorrow's Holy Grail for high-performing teams. Here's why: Men, who have traditionally held leadership roles, can be confident risk takers and negotiators. Women, on the other hand, can be great leaders who empower teams, develop high-performing talent, and think through competitive or industry-leading options and permutations. **I often refer to this healthier integrated culture as "right balanced" because that indicates an intentional shift and integration from simply including a token female voice, which is often muted and mitigated, to ensuring that a critical mass of female leaders contribute to shaping the culture and standards that drive high performance. Today, only 8% of senior executives are both strategic and have the ability to effectively execute through their teams, putting an exclamation point on the need for right-balanced teams.**

Comparing Right-Balanced and Off-Balance Teams

Off-Balance Teams	Right-Balanced Teams
Token female voice, if any	Balances an equal number of female and male perspectives as well as their skills
Mutes and mitigates female perspectives	Values male and female perspectives equally
Leads with old-world assumptions: Only the strong survive	Works toward high performance: Only the team survives
Struggles to balance execution and strategy	Implements more diverse and far-reaching skillsets that improve execution and strategy
Creates less revenue when only one gender is present	Creates more revenue with gender balance
Unsustainable and difficult to predict outcomes	Results are sustainable and more likely to match goals

Right-balanced teams also have the data on their side. As opposed to teams comprised of all women or all men, an MIT study found that one right-balanced team could create 41% more revenue than all-male or all-female teams.[3] Michel Landel of Sodexo reports that an effort to build more gender-balanced teams regularly achieved better outcomes. "We analyzed data from 50,000 managers across 90 entities around the world and the results are compelling. They clearly show that teams with a male–female ratio between 40 and 60 percent produce results that are more sustained and predictable than those of unbalanced teams."[4] When

---

[3]Dizikes, Peter, "Workplace Diversity Can Help the Bottom Line," *MIT News*, October 7, 2014. http://news.mit.edu/2014/workplace-diversity-can-help-bottom-line-1007.

[4]Landel, Michel, "Gender Balance and the Link to Performance," *McKinsey & Company*, February 2015. https://www.mckinsey.com/featured-insights/leadership/gender-balance-and-the-link-to-performance.

it comes to impacting the bottom line at the executive level, a series of studies conducted by McKinsey & Company found:

- "Companies in the top quartile for gender diversity on their executive teams were 21% more likely to experience above-average profitability."
- "Executive teams that were high-performing had more women in revenue-generating roles."
- "Companies with low representation of women and other diverse groups were 29% more likely to underperform on profitability."[5]

In addition, a study conducted over long spans of time found that women are essential for incorporating more innovation and higher profit margins. A 2012 study of 1,500 companies conducted over 15 years found that "the presence of a woman in top management amounts to creating extra market value for each firm of approximately US $44 million."[6] The conclusion is beyond dispute: Organizations that courageously commit to creating high-performance cultures led by right-balanced teams with great leaders will outpace, outmaneuver, and outperform their competition.

If making the shift to right-balanced, high-performing teams with great leaders is good for the long-term growth of employees, keeps companies on the cutting edge of innovation, and ensures higher profits, then we would expect companies that are already committed to diversity in hiring and training to be excelling in creating balanced teams with empowered women. We would expect more women to be involved in right-balanced teams, C-suites, and leadership teams and boards. We would expect more accountability for leaders to ensure that they are inspiring and empowering

---

[5] *Government of Australia: Workplace Gender Equality,* "The Business Case," https://www.wgea.gov.au/topics/workplace-gender-equality/the -business-case. Accessed February 20, 2020.
[6] Ibid.

their teams. Just a few conversations with women, and most men, who are experienced in the corporate world will tell you that this is rarely the case.

Most organizations have women and talent identification programs in place but do not realize that they are simply *adding* high performers and women to their talent pipeline and are not identifying key factors that are undermining their ability to thrive. Today's organizations are out of balance and although most companies generally want to hire more women and to allow high performers to thrive, they lack the guidance, sense of urgency, and leadership infrastructure to make necessary changes to their systems, structures, and cultures. The organizations that can shift to high-performing, right-balanced teams with great leadership will be rewarded with increased revenues, a more inspired culture, and sustainable growth. It's time to find out what we've been missing in the corporate world for so long so that we can take a meaningful step forward. Once we recognize the dynamics that are holding women and high performers back, we'll be prepared to make the shift toward fulfilling our potential and delivering superior results.

2 | Confronting Corporate Reality

"If you exclude 50% of the talent pool, it's no wonder you find yourself in a war for talent."

> —*Theresa J. Whitmarsh, executive director of the Washington State Investment Board*

Spotting and addressing the barriers that are blocking organizations from the enormous opportunities and advantages of high-performing, right-balanced teams with great leadership isn't difficult, but you have to know where to look.

Let's begin with the story of Mike, someone who embodies the experiences of many male employees in the business world.

★ ★ ★ ★ ★

Mike was smart, driven, and loved to compete, graduating from a prestigious university with honors and starring on its football team. He viewed every aspect of his life as a challenge to be the best, whether it was his relationships, college studies, or job. After graduation, a large financial services company hired Mike for a financial analyst role. Mike and his boss, a fellow college athlete, hit it off right away. Conversations about sports over cups of coffee in the hallway evolved into frequent lunches together. Although no other female colleague received similar invites to eat lunch with the boss, Mike chalked it up to his initiative, drive, and winning personality. And while female colleagues were interrupted in meetings by a few combative colleagues, Mike's boss always made sure that his views were carefully considered over their objections.

Thanks to their frequent business lunches, Mike's boss introduced him to his own boss and other peers throughout the organization. When it was time for promotions, Mike's boss advocated for his promotion, although he had only been at the company for six months. No other employee had advanced as quickly, even his hard-working colleagues Amy and Margot, who had been key contributors on his most successful projects and had been overlooked despite being with the company for 18 months.

Leadership throughout the organization began to perceive Mike in the same way his boss did: he was competent, a great leader, and had promise and potential. Mike continued to progress through the organization, making the most of every opportunity in his path, and ultimately landed in a senior executive position. A few times in his career he encountered an overly aggressive executive who used his power to subdue him and deride his performance, but Mike always managed to deflect the person's behavior or to address it head-on. He had built a big enough network to sustain him through these small hits to his career. Each conflict with a colleague or manager attempting to derail him became an opportunity to compete and win. When Mike heard reports of some colleagues, mostly women, being bullied by his latest supervisor, he found that bully's weakness and relied on his own network in order to prevail. At times Mike crossed paths with

Amy, who had advanced to a position below him in the company but surprisingly stalled in her progress despite producing excellent work. He learned that Margot had moved on to another firm and reasoned that she had been unable to handle the high-stakes pressure and risks like he could.

Mike leveraged each opportunity and relationship to prepare himself for his next step. Over time he became known throughout the company as decisive, competitive, and a risk taker. Departments and projects under his responsibility consistently produced positive outcomes. He developed a strong network outside of his company and stayed up on industry trends. If he wanted information, he simply reached out to his vast network of friends, colleagues, and acquaintances. He would leverage this information with his leadership team, from which they would generate ideas. Mike even distinguished himself by serving on a nonprofit board. After 18 years in the business, he was finally promoted to the C-suite and had reached the pinnacle of his career.

★ ★ ★ ★ ★

Mike's story stands out as a tale of success. He wisely made the most of each opportunity, took initiative, and understood when to take risks. His success is not a mirage, and he had a lot to be proud of as he looked back on his career. However, Mike and many of his colleagues were also blind to the inequalities others experienced, especially women. Mike rose to success, but how much unnecessary conflict held him and his colleagues back? How many sleepless nights did he have because he was being targeted by another leader who was levels higher than him? How many employees suffered unnecessary distress and loss of productivity because of leaders who undermined them? Can we even quantify the loss of a talented colleague like Margot or the barriers that prevented Amy from leading at a higher capacity?

It's likely that more women in leadership roles could have spotted the toxic trends holding women back at Mike's company.

This would have greatly benefited Amy and Margot, while also helping Mike and the company, since he had already demonstrated good chemistry while working with them. Despite Mike's success, his story suggests that, in many workplaces, all may not be well. That possibility comes into sharper focus with the story of Jennifer.

If we track the story of Jennifer, who shares much of the same promise and potential as Mike, we may find some unexpected barriers Mike never considered and a much better idea of the antiquated culture companies need to address with a shift toward a high-performance, right-balanced culture.

★ ★ ★ ★ ★

Jennifer graduated summa cum laude from a state college with a world-renowned engineering program. She studied hard for her grades, served as president of her sorority, raised money for childhood cancer research, and worked as a resident assistant to pay for her college expenses. She was smart, driven, and loved to make a difference, using every aspect of her life to lead teams of people to do great things. Her family even put her in charge of planning their vacations because of her attention to detail, consideration of others, and ability to meet a tight deadline.

After Jennifer's college graduation, a large engineering company hired her as an assistant engineer and placed her under Tim, a tough and very competitive boss. Tim rarely met with Jennifer one-on-one, and when he communicated about her, he sold her ideas as his own. Despite Jennifer's excellent work that earned the praise of her colleagues, Tim never advocated for Jennifer. When she asked about the requirements for a promotion, Tim told her to sit tight and it would eventually come.

After 12 months, Jennifer received a 2% raise but no promotion. She continued to work 80 hours per week, producing twice the amount of work as others while helping her colleagues succeed. She noticed that the company had a need to share information so that everyone could perform better at their jobs, so she started a study club every Monday, Wednesday, and Friday at 7:00 a.m. She developed a reputation for being a great leader of people, inspiring others, especially the few women peers she had in the organization, to be their best and to persevere through difficulty. After 18 months, Jennifer was promoted alongside other males who had only been there six months. She became a leader of more engineers and was rated a top 5% leader in their annual Gallup poll. Nevertheless, she was rotated to another role under a senior leader with a reputation throughout the organization for bullying. Although several subordinates had reported his behavior over the years, HR never followed through and those who reported the bullying behavior seemed to disappear. Jennifer soon found herself on the receiving end of his angry remarks and demeaning comments, but she resolved to work through the adversity since she lacked confidence in how HR would respond.

During Jennifer's year-end review, her boss minimized her many accomplishments and denied her a raise. Although her mentor sympathized with Jennifer, she endured another frustrating year before being rotated into another department. She had lost two years of merits and bonuses. As she focused on creating industry-leading programs and projects that earned accolades from some, she had to constantly waste her time warding off highly competitive peers who used their political influence to gain power throughout the organization. Because she was an all-around top performer in virtually every role, she repeatedly encountered envious peers who used their political influence and savvy to take her off her trajectory. Little did she know she was a threat to their existence – apparently, there was only one job for both of them.

As Jennifer rose through the ranks, she was harassed, told to perform unethical tasks, baited, subjected to character assassination, reported to bad bosses, and suffered the insults of narcissistic peers. Much of her energy was spent warding off attacks, all while attempting to lead her teams and to create inspiring cultures in these hypercompetitive environments. Through it all, she remained focused on the endgame of being a good person and doing the right thing. Toward the end of her career, she was recognized with several awards for her impact in her industry and for her inspiring leadership. She was finally promoted to the C-suite after 25 years in the business and had reached the pinnacle of her career.

★ ★ ★ ★ ★

These two stories are dramatically different and are representative of the dichotomy of today's experiences in the workplace. Mike had an instant bond with his manager over sports and shared interests that gave him an advantage whenever an imposter sought to undermine or bully him. By contrast, the barriers in Jennifer's workplace are clear. Although Mike's story hinted at the inequalities and bullying that happen in the workplace, Jennifer's experience drives home the urgency of our current situation. While selflessly building up her colleagues and working long hours to produce excellent results, she was surrounded by bullying, backstabbing, hypercompetitiveness, and verbal abuse. The leaders and HR managers who could have changed this situation were often primarily men who either didn't notice what was happening because they didn't experience the workplace the same as women or they just assumed that only the strong survive and women need to adapt. Mike was largely shielded from bullying and competitive peers through the relationship he built with a supportive boss. By the time he faced significant adversity, he was fortunate enough to have both the experience and support to work through it. Jennifer never had that benefit, and the same could be said for Amy and Margot in Mike's story.

While Mike and Jennifer each enjoyed a measure of success in their respective companies, both wasted valuable time and energy managing divisive relationships. Mike and his team lost two talented female employees who were bullied and mistreated, while

Jennifer lost valuable productivity and personal restoration time due to bullying and inequalities. Unfortunately, hypercompetitiveness, bullying, and abuse are the norm in many workplaces. Just look at the #metoo movement: the proverbial hornets' nest has been whacked, finally revealing the most sinister side of the business world and many other segments of our society.

In order to maintain a competitive edge, remain profitable, and attract top-tier talent, companies today need to foster healthier right-balanced cultures, especially among their leadership and C-suite, where standout employees like Mike and Jennifer can thrive. Companies have the talent they need, but that talent is being minimized or squandered. In fact, if we teamed up Mike and Jennifer, they would be a high-performing team with Mike's outward competitiveness, risk taking, awareness of current trends, and drive to move the business forward, coupled with Jennifer's strong leadership of people, delivering results, and willingness to develop internal mechanisms to help others perform at their very best. The two of them highlight the potential of a right-balanced high-performing leadership team. In fact, let's consider how a high-performing team that is right-balanced could produce exceptional work at a company.

Consider the story of Kris and Allen, both assigned to the company's highest-priority project. Kris was a well-respected leader who inspired teams to perform at the highest levels of the organization. Allen was widely regarded by colleagues for his attention to detail and awareness of market trends. Over the years, Kris and Allen had forged a respectful, professional relationship and had a true appreciation for each other's talents. They expected the same respect to be shown within their team. In the beginning of the project, they established ground rules for the team to follow, rules that included respectful disagreement, focusing on the end goal, pursuing the best answer instead of being right, equal representation of ideas, and no interrupting. The team knew that Kris and Allen would model these behaviors and hold them accountable as well.

As they defined the project scope, it was clear that Kris was strategic, practical, and organized. Allen brought insights, facts, and competitive information. Their team designed an innovative product, but during execution meetings, team members, including Kris and Allen, were sometimes on completely different sides of an idea. However, they always worked together to help the team find the best solution. When they disagreed, they did so behind closed doors and talked out their differences, making decisions in the best interests of the company and the project. When other senior executives tried to hijack the project, Kris and Allen joined forces to support one another in reaching their shared goal. They were a true team.

The project finished on time, on budget, and was a huge success. The entire team was recognized for leveraging their technical and collaborative skills. They didn't look to defend a position, but instead, they looked for the best answer, the one that achieved their initial goal and got the project across the finish line. Members of their team showed up each day feeling motivated and inspired, and they carried vital insights of leadership and teamwork into their future projects.

It is also worth noting that this team survived, even thrived, all while operating in a larger work environment that was toxic. Unfortunately, today's workplace cultures are not changed by one project or two leaders at a time. The first step to changing a workplace culture is to eliminate the systemic barriers that prohibit a more integrated, high-performing workplace, so that every team, not just Kris and Allen's, can perform at their highest capacity.

Confronting Reality

Today's boards and executives, the ones ultimately responsible for setting the tone, environment, and culture within organizations, are undermining the success of their companies and the well-being of those they lead by overlooking barriers that high performers and women face in the workplace. They have allowed imposters to wreak havoc on employees under their authority, fostering unhealthy competition within their teams that creates internal combustion at the expense of their employees' mental health, relationships, and productivity.

This approach has created an unnecessary churn-and-burn mentality of "may the best man win at any cost" and allowed unethical and abusive behaviors among employees, which affects everyone but especially women, who are bullied at higher rates than their male colleagues.[1] It has also promoted the wrong leaders to a company's most impactful and prestigious positions. For up-and-coming generations, the workplace is a shock to their very nature, ethics, and belief systems, especially younger women, who are technologically savvy, driven, educated, capable, and have high hopes and dreams for successful careers. This anti-bully generation is especially ill prepared for the surge of conflict and combative cultures waiting for them in the business world.

Great boards and leadership teams are keenly aware that they are ultimately accountable for not only the results but the culture of their organizations. They understand that their role is to create shareholder value, and that value is ultimately a combination of a superior brand, a high-performing CEO/leadership team, consistent financial results, the ability to remain relevant and competitive in the marketplace over time, and a highly engaged, high-performing organization.

In a company, the human assets (employees, leaders, and board members) affect every facet of shareholder value. They're an integral part of the company's brand. They create service models for how to interact with customers. They establish how products will be created and introduced. They organize to accomplish good deeds

---

[1] Agarwal, Dr. Pragya, "Here Is Why We Need to Talk about Bullying in the Workplace," *Forbes*, July 29, 2018, https://www.forbes.com/sites/pragyaagarwaleurope/2018/07/29/workplace-bullying-here-is-why-we-need-to-talk-about-bullying-in-the-work-place/#5248569d3259.

for their community. Employees are the largest expense of almost every organization, but they also ensure competitiveness in the market by generating next-gen ideas, innovation, and value. There's a competitive edge for companies who spend more time innovating in a healthy gender-balanced culture rather than repeatedly hiring and training new employees before burning through them. To make the shift, we need to ask the hard questions:

If the human side of the organization is its biggest asset, why are so few companies focusing on it?

Or, better asked, why are so many companies allowing their workplace to undermine and disenfranchise the very people who create shareholder value?

Why are companies still slow to address the disproportionate ways companies hold back women despite every available metric demonstrating their equally valuable contributions alongside men?

> In today's organizations, there is a stark difference between people who are great leaders and people who hold great titles.

A title does not a great leader make. How can leaders improve the workplace culture so that their teams shift from fragmented, winner-take-all competitions to high-performing teams leveraging each member's resources and unique talents? If a company's culture can undermine its strategy, let's consider what the culture of a high-performing workplace will look like.

The Solution: Shifting to a High-Performing Workplace

Today's workplace is at an inflection point and companies must make a shift if they want to remain competitive. High-performing men and women are converging in the workplace, and, so far, this coming together has been left, for the most part, unmanaged, creating unforeseen conflict, increasing the risk of lawsuits and diminishing company performance as top employees, and nearly all women, face barriers and waste their time managing threats from hypercompetitive colleagues. **Companies that are prepared to harness the strengths of men, women, and high performers in general will create a competitive advantage in the marketplace. Those companies that do not can expect a path toward unprecedented peril and risk.**

More women than men are earning college degrees and entering the workforce.[2] Yet very few of these women hold board, C-suite, or executive positions, because men tend to promote men and are less likely to spot the barriers that hold women back. By contrast, men, who have historically dominated board, executive, and managerial positions, can feel threatened by the advancement of women in the workplace and have been ill-prepared to lead or manage them. Couple this with the fact that abusive men are being accused of illicit wrongdoing, and the workplace has left the great male leaders on shaky ground with their female colleagues.

To maximize the positive impact men and women can have in the workplace (on profitability, sustainability, increased creativity, better products – the list goes on and on), companies need to create an *integrated high-performance, right-balanced culture* that will align and energize both high-performing men and women under great leadership. Some might argue that most companies today are already high-achieving and getting great results—just look at the stock market, overall profitability, and the worldwide market share held by U.S. companies. And yes, in some ways U.S. companies are achieving great results. They are *high-achieving*. But if you check under the hood, you'll often find organizations that are wrought with

---

[2]Napolitano, Janet, "Women Earn More College Degrees and Men Still Earn More Money," *Forbes*, September 9, 2014, https://www.forbes.com/sites/janetnapolitano/2018/09/04/women-earn-more-college-degrees-and-men-still-earn-more-money/#2480285339f1.

chaos and inefficient human resource management. Their internal cultures and performance management systems are overly competitive, churn through their employees, and waste the many talents that women and high performers can bring to the table. The true story, the one hidden behind all the figures, is that their outcomes are typically created at the expense of the people doing the work.

But there are also *high-performing* companies, few and far between in corporate America, achieving results through healthier methods: they have high-performing teams maximizing their employees in sustainable ways. In these workplaces, gender-balanced teams work collaboratively and inspire the highest quality and innovation. They are engaged, productive, and encouraged about the future. They think short-, medium-, and long-term and never waiver on their core mission or vision. They have great leaders who earn the trust of their teams and celebrate their peers' successes because they hold themselves and their teams accountable to high standards. While the status quo may lead to good results, companies willing to make this shift to gender-balanced high-performing teams could achieve better, longer-lasting results while also giving their employees higher job satisfaction and quality of life.

The primary difference between a company that is high-achieving and one that is high-performing is *how* the company accomplishes the results through their employees – their most prized asset. A high-*achieving* company culture is much more sinister and short-term and could cost shareholders billions of dollars each year. A high-*performing* culture has the opportunity to create shareholder value over the long term and maximizes the use of its available assets. High-performing cultures recognize the many benefits of including more women in leadership roles, holding leaders accountable for their development of high performers, and reviewing how leaders are promoted by implementing a plan to make a shift happen.

The accountability for beginning this shift rests on the boards and executive leadership.

3

The Barriers That Hold Back High Performers and Women

"In the future there will be no female leaders. There will just be leaders."

— *Sheryl Sandberg,* Lean In

Today's ambitious imposter leaders have created the barriers to our future high-performing teams and organizations. To create the high-performing organization of the future, we must first recognize and remove the barriers that are impeding the company's ability to fully leverage high-performing talent, especially women. Only then will organizations have the opportunity to redesign high-performing teams in which women can thrive alongside men. Consider the following few examples based on mentees I've coached in the workplace. While plenty of men have shared these experiences, I guarantee you that *every* woman with experience in corporate America will relate to these examples:

31

The college graduate: Bella just graduated summa cum laude with a degree in finance from a state university and has landed a job at a reputable firm. In her training class of eight, four are women and four are men. Over the next five weeks they will train together every day, eight hours per day, before they are assigned to a team. The men in the class finish every assignment first and then spend the remainder of the time chatting with the instructor about sports. The women finish after the men and proceed to talk among themselves. One day, Bella suggests a new approach to the training class. It would create efficiency by eliminating one whole week of training, putting them into the business unit sooner. Jeff, one of the class-mates, stated that he was thinking the exact same thing and thinks the instructor should do it. The instructor thanks Jeff for his idea, which is implemented and works exactly as Bella said it would. Jeff gets invited by the trainer to present the new approach to a group of senior managers. When the class is finished, Jeff is assigned to a top up-and-coming male manager. Bella gets assigned to a good manager. Six months later, Jeff gets promoted. Bella does not.

On the fast track: Isabel is a top-performing senior manager who leads a high-impact department, manages eight people directly, and is on the company high-potential list. She recently returned from speaking at a conference, where she unveiled her company's new product line, designed by her team. This landed an article in a magazine in which she was quoted. The CEO of the company reads the article and sends her a nice e-mail thanking her for a great job. He mentions that he has been hearing great things about her and looks forward to a one-on-one in the near future.

Isabel's current boss, James, is very supportive of her as well. But soon, everything begins to change. Unbeknownst to her, two of her high-potential team members are invited to meet with Steve, a higher-level leader from a different department. In these meetings, Steve asks about their department, the key project that is just getting ready to launch, and their career aspirations.

Soon after these meetings, Isabel's boss starts acting differently toward her, asking for more specifics about her department. Are these efficiency numbers correct? Does she really save that much money on the budget? Are the new products ready to launch? Then he starts disengaging publicly in staff meetings. If Isabel speaks up, he doesn't look at her.

Steve is rotated into their business unit without any explanation. Isabel speaks to her mentor about the situation – she's confused and doesn't know what changed. When she asks James about it, he changes the subject. Then, her mentor informs her she is being taken off the high-potential list, and there has even been discussion that she is not an effective leader. She hears through the rumor mill that there are big issues in her department and that her people were even seeking out help from Steve instead of from her. The plan soon comes into focus – they are going to take the department away from her and give it to Steve, doubling the size of his department and reassigning the top company initiative to him.

The high-performing executive: Lauren is finally promoted to an executive position. From the time she entered her first job out of college, it has been her dream to land this position. She worked tirelessly over her 20-year career and her resume contains a list of industry-leading accomplishments. She has consistently been a highly rated leader in her industry per Gallup's annual survey and is admired by her peers as trustworthy and collaborative. She is ethical and stays out of the political fray. She advocates for her team and is beloved by most everyone in her department.

She knows that Amber, one of the other executives, wanted the job that Lauren recently received. One thing about Amber is that she has the ambition but lacks the skills central to taking the department, and the organization, where it needs to go.

Two years go by, reporting lines change, and Lauren begins reporting to Amber. For Lauren, this is a huge red flag. Amber achieved her position, one of the highest in the organization, through stealth and subterfuge. Her path is littered with people she used and then discarded, but for some reason, the senior leaders love her. She has gravitas, connections, and a history of bold moves.

Soon after she becomes Lauren's boss, Amber "challenges" her to come up with a whole new product line . . . in four weeks. "If you are the rock star everyone says you are," Amber claims, "this shouldn't be a problem." In the past, one new product took over 18 months to create.

How was Lauren ever going to do this well? Even if she worked her typical 75 hours per week, she could not redirect the resources needed to accomplish this BHAG (big hairy aggressive goal).

The four weeks come and go, and while Lauren's team is well on their way to creating a new product line, they simply need more time. Amber begins expressing her discontentment with Lauren to the other executives, using as her main complaint Lauren's "inability to hit production targets," and eventually Lauren is squeezed out of the company.

★★★★★

Like Bella, most women out of college are competing for that first promotion, yet consistently are overlooked by male executives.[1] Others, like Isabel, are being confronted by overcompetitive peers who use their time and energy to discredit top performers whose only goal is the expansion of their corporate footprint and power. And then there's Lauren, who finally makes it to the executive ranks only to be undermined by unethical tactics.

The career paths of women in corporate America are full of land mines, from their first role in the organization all the way up to the top (if they're fortunate enough to survive that long into the journey). These land mines are palpable, documented, and very

---

[1]Jingcong, Zhao, "New Research: Men Promote Men and Women Promote Women," *PayScale*, May 3, 2018, https://www.payscale.com/career-news/2018/05/new-research-promotion-gap.

real, and they keep women from performing to their full potential, derail their careers, and block them from successful trajectories. The women in these examples just touch the tip of the proverbial iceberg, as women and increasing numbers of men in the corporate world also face bullying, abusive language, and harassment. When facing these barriers and abuses from a superior, women rarely have a viable recourse to address the situation.

Unfortunately for women, they cannot fully understand these perils until they've had personal experience with them. The issue quickly becomes overwhelming – one they haven't been prepared to handle. Few navigate these perils successfully, because they rarely understand why they are happening or what they can do to remedy the situation.

Such situations leave most women asking what they did wrong, but the reality is that it's not the woman's issue to fix.

The solution begins in the boardroom and the C-suite.

Where the Shift Must Begin

Since Sheryl Sandberg's groundbreaking book *Lean In* burst onto the scene in 2013, women have entered the workforce armed with the pearls of wisdom and encouragement found on those pages. Fortunately, one end result is that women have raised their voices, illuminated the toxicity of the workplace, and shared the way corporate culture churns through female leaders and creates situations that are unhealthy for both men and women. In this age of greater transparency, when women are speaking up, it has become clear: if companies want to truly maximize the value of all their employees and co-workers, both women and men, they must first identify the systemic barriers in their organizations that keep workplaces high-achieving instead of high-performing.

The numbers that bear witness to these barriers are staggering, as you'll see in the following data, but the specific barriers leading to these abuses have not been fully illuminated until recently. According to a McKinsey/LeanIn study, women are increasingly articulating the hostile and abusive situations they encounter in the workplace.[2] These situations happen at every level – from the mail-room to the boardroom – and their pervasiveness has achieved epidemic proportions. Even more surprising, it also happens to men.

But wait, some of you might be saying. *An epidemic? Isn't that overstating it a bit?*

I hear you, and it's a good question, so let's consider the definitions for the words *epidemic* and *majority* and compare them with the current situation.

If you look at the definition of an epidemic, *The Merriam-Webster Dictionary* states, " . . . the rule of thumb for meningococcal disease, for example, is that an attack rate in excess of 15 cases per 100,000 people for two consecutive weeks constitutes a sizable epidemic . . . " And if you consider the definition for a large majority, you will find the following: "When voting, a large majority can be defined as an unquestionable number such that there's no point in demanding a recount, or something like 60%."

Meanwhile, 75% of women and 35% of men in the workplace have been subjected to abuse. Over 70% of workers have been bullied. And **70% of those who report abuse have been retaliated against**.[3]

[2]Huang, Jess, Alexis Krivkovich, Irina Starikova, Lareina Yee, and Delia Zanoschi, "Women in the Workplace 2019," *McKinsey & Company*, October 2019, https://www.mckinsey.com/featured-insights/gender-equality/women-in-the-workplace-2019.

[3]Agarwal, Dr. Pragya, "Here Is Why We Need to Talk about Bullying in the Workplace," *Forbes*, July 29, 2018, https://www.forbes.com/sites/pragyaagarwaleurope/2018/07/29/workplace-bullying-here-is-why-we-need-to-talk-about-bullying-in-the-work-place/#5248569d3259.

Reported Abuse at Work	
Women	75%
Men	35%

These numbers prove that the barriers are real and pervasive and contribute to the epidemic of a toxic workplace for the majority of women and many men in this country.

So, what are these barriers? Let's consider the three most common and then we'll review their consequences for organizations.

Barrier 1: Pervasive Aggression/Micro-Inequities

Micro-inequities are "ways in which individuals are singled out, overlooked, ignored, or otherwise discounted based on an unchangeable characteristic such as race or gender."[4] Micro-inequities, micro-affirmations, and micro-advantages all fall within the broader category of micro-messaging. All represent the three ways we send subtle messages negatively or positively.[5]

According to a 2007 Korn Ferry report, micro-inequities have massive and harmful impacts on organizations. Over 2 million managers and professionals (both men and women) leave their jobs each year due to unfair practices in the workplace. However, the 2018 McKinsey/LeanIn study found that women who encounter workplace aggression are three times more likely to think about leaving their jobs.[6]

---

[4]Find Words, "Gender," https://findwords.info/term/gender.
[5]Find Words, "Micro-Inequity," https://findwords.info/term/micro-inequity.
[6]Krivkovich, Alexis, Marie-Claude Nadeau, Kelsey Robinson, Nicole Robinson, Irina Starikova, and Lareina Yee, "Women in the Workplace 2018," *McKinsey & Company,* October 2018, https://www.mckinsey.com/featured-insights/gender-equality/women-in-the-workplace-2018.

Micro-inequities, also referred to as pervasive aggressions, can often seem inconsequential, but they are actually impactful and keep women and high-performers from performing their best. Whether it's having a bad boss, being talked over in a meeting, not receiving credit for work or ideas, or being outpromoted, these situations are relatively easy to identify and even easier to address in the workplace.

The key is to identify when these situations are happening and to connect the issue to the originator – the perpetrator of the aggression. I cannot emphasize this enough: the originator of the aggression needs to be identified and confronted. Once these individuals are exposed, it is much easier to mitigate their behavior. Identifying these pervasive inequities and aggressions is the first step in creating a shift in your culture and setting the stage for all employees – both men and women – to shine.

Barrier 2: Workplace Targeting and Bullying

Bullies in the workplace often target individuals who appear to be the most competent, smart, and self-assured. This kind of targeting is rooted in the bully's perception of someone as a threat to their own status or influence. Most states now have laws against bullying in schools, but the workplace has yet to achieve this standard. **As more men and women from the anti-bullying generation enter the workforce, bullying presents an increasing risk for corporations. Unlike previous generations, today's young people have been taught not to accept bullying, and they are less likely to stay in an organization where it is tolerated.**

Today, a majority of bullying in the workplace is directed at women. **The Workplace Bullying Institute found that 70% of bullies were men, who targeted women 65% of the time. In addition, 30% of the bullies were women, who**

target other women 67% of the time.[7] The key takeaway: in the workplace, women are getting bullied – from both men and women – a large majority of the time. Yet, men are also suffering from the pervasiveness of bullying in the workplace. The Workplace Bullying Institute also found in a 2017 survey that Hispanic and Black workers were more likely to be bullied,[8] and a study conducted by Georgia State University noted that African Americans were more likely than whites to be bullied at work.[9] The dynamics of race in workplace bullying conversations cannot be overlooked, but as of this writing we lack a large body of research on the topic.[10] This book will focus on the benefits of selecting high-performing leaders, high potentials, and women in the workplace (as relates to gender balance), and this includes men and women of color, although, due to lack of studies on the subject, we are unable to definitively substantiate the impact.

Bullying is even more destructive and widespread than aggression situations, and it normally occurs when one person or a group of colleagues is targeted by one individual. Situations involving bullying stretch out over longer periods of time and require much more energy and stamina to combat. Bullying is more complex and can have a much wider impact than micro-inequities, stopping not just with the person being bullied but also affecting large swathes of the

---

[7]Namie, Dr. Gary, "2017 WBI U.S. Workplace Bullying Survey," Workplace Bullying Institute, June 2017, https://www.workplacebullying.org/wbiresearch/wbi-2017-survey/.

[8]Ibid.

[9]Kummerow, Kiersten, "Workplace Bullying, Perceived Job Stressors, and Psychological Distress: Gender and Race Differences in the Stress Process," *Social Science Research*, July 2017, https://www.sciencedirect.com/science/article/abs/pii/S0049089X16305087.

[10]Feijó Fernando R., Débora D. Gräf, Neil Pearce, and Anaclaudia G. Fassa, "Risk Factors for Workplace Bullying: A Systematic Review," *International Journal of Environmental Research and Public Health*, June 16, 2019, https://www.ncbi.nlm.nih.gov/pmc/articles/PMC6603960/.

organization and its culture. Since it's often designed to minimize the impact and reputation of individuals by assassinating their character, bullying could have long-lasting effects on their mental health and their careers.

Barrier 3: Workplace Abuse

The most egregious situations in the workplace are categorized as abuse (sexual, physical, or harassment). Other examples include CEOs with unethical standards, a boss who sets up employees for failure so that they can be fired, or employees who are willing to lie in order to have their co-workers demoted.

These types of toxic behaviors can derail an individual's future and can have profound negative effects that are not limited to the individual or organization but can leach out into the industry grapevine, affecting the individual's ability to obtain future employment. Often, abusive situations will end up involving federal regulators or other segments of the justice system.

For organizations, abusive situations prove most harmful to individuals and carry the highest level of legal risk. Abuse acted out at the corporate level may even be hidden when an organization starts a women's initiative as a cover for age and gender discrimination. These abuses typically happen at the leadership or executive level, but can harm anyone in the organization.

The Devastating Results of Workplace Abuse

These illicit barriers are a reflection of the single largest challenge within company culture: to eradicate abusive norms that create a cesspool of toxicity, which in turn erodes a company's talent and overall success. The role of boards, executives, leaders, and human resource professionals is to create value for shareholders or owners.

Allowing a toxic workplace puts your organization at risk and is one of the most significant impediments to creating a high-performance organization.

Here are just a few of the practical, negative effects of these abusive or undermining barriers on your company:

Eliminates the company's talent pool, especially women. Imposters abuse, bully, and eliminate your high-performing and high-potential employees, prompting many to leave or take themselves out of the running for critical roles. This removes key individuals from your talent pool and is especially impactful on women, as evidenced by the numbers we've reviewed on bullying.

Toxicity rises to the highest levels of your organization. Because imposters are adept at navigating the political landscape of your organization, they rise to the top. Once there, they expect others to play the same game, and therefore the toxic culture not only continues, but becomes expected and exacerbated throughout the company, from the highest positions to entry-level ones.

Increases turnover and expenses. Whenever an employee leaves, the associated costs to the organization are 1.5 times their salary.[11] With an estimated 2 million employees leaving their jobs each year due to toxic managers and workplaces, that equates to an enormous cost to shareholders.

Primarily targets women, who are generally not equipped or trained to handle abuse. For men, managing these situations is much more innate because these barriers are typical in man-to-man settings. Although men have suffered under bullies and self-serving leaders, they traditionally have a disagreement, resolve it, and move on. For women, it's not that easy. Women tend to personalize the abuse, taking on misplaced responsibility,

---

[11]Korn/Ferry International, "The Cost of Employee Turnover Due to Failed Diversity Initiatives in the Workplace: The Corporate Leavers Survey 2007," https://www.kornferry.com/institute/download/download/id/17144/aid/397.

and then attempt to resolve an issue that's unresolvable because of the toxic environment. This challenge will only increase as graduates from generations that emphasized anti-bullying advance in the workplace.

Creates an environment where promotions are given based on faulty criteria. When used internally, these barriers turn into a game of power – that is, may the strongest man win. Promoting the loudest person who acts in control is a false positive for leadership and leaves some of the highest performers who drive results out of the running for top positions. Aggressiveness and gravitas tend to be false positives for evaluating effective employees and leaders based on qualitative measures. The new high-performing organizations will use qualitative *and* quantitative methods for selecting high performers.

Costs companies money and brand equity. The scope of today's digital world means that barriers can cost companies more than just money. Bad press, reduced sales, high performers who steer away from applying for critical positions – all of these are monetary risks to employers and shareholders when the barriers to high performance remain in place. When there's a war for talent in corporate America, don't expect top performers to tolerate bullying and derailing behaviors for long. Companies also need to recognize that women, as a growth market, equate to the fifth-largest economy in the world and make over 90% of household purchasing decisions.[12] Have you ever tried to sell your products to a woman who has found out your company is abusive toward women? It is nearly impossible. As consumers, women have really long memories, deep wallets, and will begin to take their money elsewhere as long as these barriers remain in your organization.

---

[12]Silversetin, Michaeal J. and Kate Sayre, "The Female Economy," *Harvard Business Review*, September 2009, https://hbr.org/2009/09/the-female-economy.

Creates toxic leaders with destructive values. Typically, these individuals are rising through the ranks or sit on your executive team and are therefore some of your highest-paid individuals. If you think of them as a value (the quality they bring vs. the cost), these individuals carry a negative value to your organization. For example, if a toxic leader makes $350,000 each year in compensation and they eliminate a high performer from your organization who has typically driven revenues equal to five times their annual compensation of $200,000, your company just lost at least $1 million of revenue *in one year* from that one employee alone, not to mention the ongoing costs and lost revenues that will become amplified due to retaining the toxic leader.

Misuses company influence for individual benefit. Toxic players, both men and women, are simply using your company as a platform to carry out their psychological warfare on others. But because they manage up so well, they feed the egos of bosses and other executives. Unfortunately, these executives fail to realize they are being played as well, diminishing their own credibility in the organization. When employees leverage the company for their own gain, a host of long-term problems arises, including unethical behavior. Unethical behavior is at the epicenter of the individualist's playbook and can lead to misappropriation of funds, executive or business decisions made on false or exaggerated information, or reporting of false information to government agencies.

This kind of behavior also leads to leaders being less respectful of employees' nonwork commitments,[13] a loss of innovation, wasted time, high turnover and absenteeism, increased apathetic compliance, detachment, impaired problem-solving skills, low morale, and more health problems – and if all of those weren't

---

[13]Brooke, Chad, "Toxic Leaders Offer Short-Term Benefits, But Long-Term Problems," *Business News Daily*, June 18, 2017, https://www.businessnewsdaily.com/10014-toxic-leaders-problems.html.

enough, toxic leaders also expose the organization to greater PR risks and other serious consequences.[14]

Creates financial and legal risks for employers. I'm convinced that new laws will soon be introduced that will make bullying in the workplace illegal. With the #metoo movement alone, sexual discrimination reports to the EEOC increased 50% in 2018 and over $70 million was awarded in damages. With anti-bullying school laws enacted in virtually every state, workplace laws are soon to follow as the students from those schools enter universities and the workforce.

Are you starting to see how costly these barriers are to your company? Can you see how insidious and prevalent they are in your corporate culture?

Here's the good news: shifting the rules is not as hard as you think.

It begins with addressing workplace bullying and other pervasive toxic behaviors.

Removing the Barriers That Impede High Performance

To make the shift, leaders at the top must start with a concrete plan to eliminate the barriers that block their company from creating a high-performance culture.

The reality I've found is that it requires real leadership to take action.

★★★★★

Serena had finally made it. After 24 years, she was hired for her dream role in the C-suite. Throughout her career, she had

---

[14]CMOE, "Why Toxic Leaders Will Ruin a Workplace," Accessed September 25, 2019, https://cmoe.com/blog/why-toxic-leaders-will-ruin-a-workplace/.

encountered ups and downs, good people and bad people, and had vowed to herself that if she ever made it into this seat, she was going to make it better for the current employees and the next generation so that they wouldn't have to encounter the same sinister side of business that she had. She had encountered too many individuals who had achieved critical leadership roles in the organization despite not caring about their teams, their peers, or their leaders. They were simply out to win at all costs.

Serena wasn't like that. She thought of leadership as the highest honor in an organization, and she spent time developing and mentoring her team members and speaking at events in her industry. She was ethical, intelligent, driven, and a team player. Whatever she achieved in her career came about because of her ability to make sure that everyone on the team was able to leverage their talents. She was the leader, but it was her leadership of the team that created her extraordinary success.

Being a team player in a company that often promoted individuals who were solely out for themselves wasn't easy. She encountered imposter leaders who were narcissistic, who lied about others to discredit them so they could get ahead, and who even strategically manipulated the organization and took credit for other people's work to senior leadership in order to expand their own responsibilities. Serena's integrity had been brought into question simply because someone else lied about something she never said.

Now she had made it to the top, and it was her opportunity to develop and promote leaders with the right skill sets. Serena knew from her own experience that high-performing teams were led by high-performing leaders and in order to increase the performance of the organization, they needed to find, cultivate, and promote high performers. She envisioned a diverse group of leaders – diverse in that they would think differently, have different experiences, were team players aligned to the purpose and mission of the company, and were trusted by their peers and teams.

Serena's goal of diversity should have been easy. After all, the company had defined diversity as hiring more women and people of different ethnicities and had even made it a priority. But little progress had been made, despite the fact that the initiative had begun over 15 years ago!

During her first meeting with fellow C-suite executives, she questioned the slow progress.

"What are our goals this year when it comes to hiring more diversely?" she asked.

The room was silent. Even the chief human resources officer, Heather, was set back by her line of questions.

"Goals?" Heather asked, clearly puzzled. "What goals? You can't put a goal on diversity, can you?"

Serena heard a few chuckles in the room. Heather was clearly walking the line between being serious and sarcastic.

"Well," Serena continued, "do we have goals on diverse hiring?"

Again, no response. She then asked if they had an initiative to help women succeed in the organization; finally she received an answer.

"Yes," Heather said. "Yes, we do. It is an organic approach. They figure out what they need and bring their requests to us."

"Are there any guidelines for them to follow with these requests?" Serena asked.

Again, silence. Heather finally spoke. "The board felt we should do something but did not have any specific goals for us. The board felt we needed to do something but they really aren't pushing it."

Serena's head reeled as she sat at the boardroom table, questioning her company's dedication to diversity in hiring. If there are no goals, how can they move from where they are today to where they need to be? Heather claimed that women could receive additional training and resources through an organic process of asking for what they need, but what did that even mean? Organic? How does a woman who is in the trenches know what she needs?

★★★★★

Without the board establishing goals and the C-suite determining how to achieve them, the company will continue at its current pace – a company that looks like many others in the United States, with a small number of women in the C-suite surrounded by a toxic culture dominated by managers with sharp elbows. There will continue to be unequal gender representation in leadership roles, little to no diversity, and many barriers to high performance.

As a senior leader in the organization, Serena experienced the company culture firsthand. She also mentored and sponsored many women – and men – in the organization. Neither was able to invest their unique talents into projects, relationships, or the company mission because they were too focused on organizational politics.

Serena left that meeting with more questions than answers: "How can I help move our organization from high-achieving to high-performing? What will it take to get more women into the boardroom, C-suites, and director-level positions?"

In other words, how can a business's performance infrastructure be changed?

According to the Workplace Bullying Institute (WBI), an organization established in 1997 "dedicated to the eradication of workplace bullying," the more you expose inequities, bullying, and abuse in the workplace, the more chances you have to significantly change or reduce the toxic culture in your organization. But it requires a defined program and a village to implement it – executives, human resources management, leaders, and the women and men on the receiving end of the toxic behavior. Knowing and understanding the three different barriers discussed earlier can help you understand and prepare for what is happening, allowing you to navigate these minefields with less stress and greater self-confidence while helping you to enjoy your life while worrying less about work.

If you are on the board or executive team at an organization, beware: if you allow bullying and abuse in the workplace, you are going down a dangerous road. You are running serious risks that will lead to underperforming individuals and, possibly, litigation.

For companies, executives, and human resource departments, the times are changing. This is a warning shot across the bow for companies that allow bullying and abuse in the workplace. The more these are reported, the more risk you have as an organization. Getting in front of the issue is critical for survival.

You simply must begin to address your culture's toxic employees and leaders. You must redefine expectations and rules.

It's not too late. You can still make the shift to a high-performing environment where the best leaders rise to the top and that allows men and women to flourish together. But you have to start now.

The key to a pervasive and sweeping change is twofold: top-down change and accountability from the board and C-suite and creating expectations of high-performing, courageous women and men – or, better yet, teams and groups – to speak up and to become catalysts for change. When the perpetrators of inequity are held accountable, new cultural norms begin to develop and the culture will begin to shift to an integrated, right-balanced high-performing organization where *both* men and women can thrive. Yet, they cannot do this without the support and infrastructure already in place.

Creating change in an organization takes only one person in the C-suite who has the courage to become an agent of change. It starts with identifying and removing the barriers that allow toxic behaviors – and leaders – to persist. Let's take a look at the most toxic behaviors and determine how pervasively they are accepted in your organization. Then, we'll look at steps you can take to lead your organization through transformational change.

Are you ready?

Let's do this.

PART II

Removing the Barriers

4

Removing Pervasive Aggression and Inequity Tactics from Your Organization

"When a good person meets a bad system, the system always wins."
—Frank Voehl

Taylor recently joined the company after graduating from a highly regarded university. She is smart, driven, respected, and is viewed as an up-and-coming talent at her company. While she sits at her cubical, Zack, one of the other individuals she started with, walks by and says "Hey!" to Taylor, then he stops at Corey's cube. Corey stands up, they bro hug, make some hand gestures, slap each other on the back, and talk about how they cannot wait to go golfing with Luke, their manager, on Sunday. Golfing? Taylor was never invited.

Taylor walks into her next meeting with some of the key managers: Anthony, Jim, Mike, and Doug, all from her division. Taylor is there to provide a project overview, along with her co-lead, Alex. Taylor kicks off the meeting and states that they researched the project's original direction, but that she and Alex were thinking that there was a more cost-effective way to accomplish their goals with an even greater result. Mike jumps in and states that that was not what they were asked to do. They were instructed to come back with a plan.

Alex, Taylor's co-lead, responds to Mike and shares his perspective about why he thinks this direction makes sense. He reiterates what Taylor had said, almost word for word. Heads began to nod around the table. Mike nods as well, leaning back with his arms crossed.

Taylor picks up where Alex left off, continuing to propose and explain their rationale. As Taylor is talking, Jim talks over her and asks Alex a question. Taylor stops talking. Mike then looks directly at Taylor and challenges her, asking her for specifics on how this would get done. When Taylor begins to talk through the plan, Doug jumps in, offering a solution they should consider. Mike needs to wrap up the meeting because he has another meeting coming up. He instructs Alex to come back and propose the plan for his new solution.

Mike then looks toward the men around the room. "I'll see you guys at lunch."

This happens every day in corporate America. Most individuals know there's something wrong about these interactions, but might not be able to put their finger on what's actually happening. All the while, these exchanges chip away at the very foundation of a high-performing company culture and open the door to micro-bullying or micro-inequities, affecting the ability of women and high performers to rise through an organization.

Recognizing when these occur, and addressing them, is the first step to creating a more balanced playing field and moving the company into a high-performance culture.

What Do Micro-Inequities Look Like?

Here are the most pervasive aggressions or micro inequities Taylor experienced in the earlier story. In fact, they are experienced by most women and undermined high performers in today's under-performing workplace:

Exclusion. Excluding someone is a subtle way of telling them that they are not an important part of the team or activity. Some examples are excluding women (or a high-performing man who is perceived as a threat) from a meeting, one-gender lunches, or holding all-male golf games on Sunday afternoons. Exclusion can also be even more subtle – for example, having nicknames and special handshakes, or turning their back to an individual when speaking to someone else.

Dismissing. Dismissing an idea by a woman but accepting it when it is paraphrased or reiterated word for word by a man.

Talking over. Women speak to share and establish connection whereas men speak to achieve power. Maybe you're not convinced this is a real occurrence? In a George Washington University study, men interrupted women 33% more than they interrupted other men.[1] While men may experience occasional interruptions, women are more likely to face them regularly.

---

[1] Shore, Leslie. "Gal Interrupted," *Forbes*, January 3, 2017, https://www.forbes.com/sites/womensmedia/2017/01/03/gal-interrupted-why-men-interrupt-women-and-how-to-avert-this-in-the-workplace/# 1323123e17c3.

Challenging women and not men. Women are challenged by men five times more often than men are and are expected to have all of the answers, putting pressure on women to perform above and beyond their male counterparts.

Aggressive or passive body language. Individuals will use this tactic to throw others off their game and redirect the attention to themselves. They will use overzealous staring tactics, fold their arms, make loud sighs, roll their eyes, check e-mail, or even close their eyes to show disengagement and reduce the presenter's confidence.

What Women and High Performers Can Do

The first step is to become aware of when these things are happening. The second step is to plan how you will approach these kinds of situations – it's always best to be ready ahead of time. Talk to human resources early in your employment, whether or not you have experienced micro-inequities, and determine how these situations should be handled if they happen in your workplace. If HR doesn't have a clearly defined set of rules, suggest developing them together. If you do not have a strong HR department willing to work through this with you, here are some basic approaches to get you started:

Exclusion. The first step is to find out what will be discussed at any particular gathering (a meeting, lunch, or out-of-hours gathering) and what they hope to accomplish. If you determine that you could make a positive contribution or impact and should play a role in any of them, send the organizer an e-mail inviting them to get together to discuss the meeting itself. Once together, confirm your understanding of the meeting agenda and then present your rationale for inclusion. Be open to the fact that they may present information you were not aware of. Your goal is to determine whether your perspective should be represented at the meeting and, if so, request that you be included. If they decline to invite you, ask for notes from the meeting and inform your boss of the situation at your next one-on-one.

In this situation, Taylor should have looked at Mike and asked to continue to be included in the creation of the plan. If she did not feel comfortable asking in the room, she should have stopped by Mike's office and asked him personally.

Your biggest concern with exclusion should focus on times a group gets together to discuss or to make decisions on a topic that affects *your responsibilities*. It's one thing to feel left out, but it's another for colleagues to hold a meeting on a topic within your scope of responsibility. It's important for you to be able to distinguish between the two.

Dismissing women and high performers. If your original credit gets lost in the conversation, simply thank the person who is receiving the final credit for being a good team member and supporting you. Without them, your idea might not have taken hold. If there is a project that is a direct result of your initial proposal, ask or insist on being included in co-leading the team as you have given it a lot of thought and look forward to contributing.

There are several factors that can initiate the dismissing of a woman's idea in particular. Sometimes it takes multiple people to share a thought before there is enough support to move the idea forward. In business, this happens more than anyone thinks, so be aware of the power of multiple mentions – but also be prepared to voice your involvement. In the case of a high performer who is dismissed or overlooked, that is most likely due to a colleague feeling threatened by the high performer's rise within the company.

Talking over women. Interrupting or talking over someone is a power play and is disrespectful to everyone else in the room, especially the one speaking. There is no room for this in a high-performing culture, and leadership must work hard to eliminate it. If you are talked over, it is appropriate to interrupt the interrupter and simply tell the person interrupting you that you need one more minute to make your point, after which you would gladly give them time to make theirs. The key is to be respectful but assertive and pointed.

Overchallenging women and high performers. There are several ways to handle being overchallenged. First and foremost, be prepared. The great news is that most women and high performers already think strategically, map through different scenarios and impact, and can talk details. Being prepared for any question that may come your way is the hallmark of any top performer.

Second, maintain your composure. Don't let the endless stream of questions throw you off your game. Getting upset restricts blood flow to your brain, reducing your ability to think clearly. You can literally keep a clear head by staying composed and not letting emotions creep in. Also, if one person is barraging you with questions, it is probably less about truly understanding what you are bringing to the table and more about grandstanding or trying to assume your power in a meeting.

Third, turn being overchallenged into a positive. Thank the person asking the questions. Use it as an opportunity to share what you know or your depth of thinking on a particular topic. For women who are being overchallenged more than their male counterparts, they should ask their team members or peers to jump in with their thoughts and ideas, both men and women.

Fourth, manage the overchallenging by identifying it. Let the challengers know that they are asking a lot of questions. If the questions are coming from one person in particular, consider opening up the floor and allowing others to voice their opinions – both positive and critical – and questions as well. This will take the spotlight off of the person asking the questions and redirect the conversation to a more productive one for all involved.

Fifth, always get to the heart of the concern or challenge for this one individual. Ask questions like, "What is your worst fear?" or "As the head of x, what is your greatest concern?" Then solicit the team's perspective to determine if this person's concerns represent the team's concerns.

Sixth, ignore aggressive or passive body language. The key to curbing others who use these tactics is to simply understand what they are doing and ignore it. It is the job of the leaders in the room to address this individual. Simply ignore their posturing and need for attention by directing your energy toward engaging the others in the room.

What High-Performing Leaders Can Do

As a leader creating a high-performing culture, your role in a group meeting is to help focus on the goal at hand while maximizing the talent in the room. We can all agree that great discussion is part of that process, but bullying a woman or a high performer is not. If you witness any of the pervasive or micro-aggressions we've discussed, it is your role to take note, shift the balance in the room, and create a higher-performing environment.

Members of high-performing teams question and challenge each other all the time, but they do so with respect. When you focus on the topic at hand and eliminate the posturing and political maneuvering, you elicit a more productive use of everyone's time.

Here are a few tactics to keep the discussion focused on high-performance solutions:

Exclusion. When you are invited to a meeting, look at the list of attendees. Is it balanced in terms of gender? Are there any key high performers missing who could add to your effectiveness? Look for opportunities to include a balance of women and men in the meeting, and individuals who offer different perspectives.

Dismissing. If a woman or high performer initiates an idea in a meeting and you notice another person receiving the credit, thank the woman with the original idea immediately and publicly.

Being talked over. When interruptions occur, let the interrupter know that you are interested in what he or she has to say and ask them to hold off on their statement or question until the original speaker is finished. To show the true power of support in the workplace, if you also notice a woman trying to speak up but being overshadowed, find an opportunity to ask for her opinion, particularly on a topic where she will shine. This action will help build her confidence and present you as a leader in the room.

Challenging women, not men. If you notice an overzealous individual consistently challenging women in the room, immediately step in and stop the inconsiderate behavior, particularly if the questions or statements are meant to demean or discredit the individual, or if that person is using the meeting to create their own center of power. Once you've interrupted their flow, look for patterns to their questions and attempt to group them into a few main concerns, and then clarify with the person in the meeting.

You could say something like, "Mike, you have a lot of questions for Mary and we need to distill them down to a few main areas of concern. What I'm hearing is that you feel that this project is a risk to client loyalty goals. Is that correct? If so, what are your two main concerns?" This provides Mary time to breathe and puts the onus back on the individual asking the questions. It will become clear very quickly if the person was asking the questions to discredit the speaker, take on newfound power, or because they had genuine concerns.

Aggressive and passive body language. All leaders in the room have the responsibility to ensure that everyone is engaged and contributing. The best way to mitigate posturing in any meeting is to set the tone by clearly articulating the purpose of the meeting and what you are looking for from each participant. If you have a few leaders in the room who have displayed aggressive or passive body language in the past, set a few ground rules. If, after articulating expectations, you notice a leader using aggressive or passive body language, first try to reengage them by asking them a direct question. If they continue with the posturing or fail to reengage, focus your energy on the others in the meeting and address the leader's behavior with them afterwards, behind closed doors.

Moving an organization from being a war on talent to one of high performance doesn't solely depend on how women and high performers handle challenging situations like the scenarios outlined above. While women and high performers can use these strategies to increase their effectiveness and to address some of the barriers and problems in an organization, leadership from the top can eradicate these unwanted aggressions. Simple action from HR and executives can free teams to think of ways to fulfill their mission, rather than how to survive their next encounter with a colleague sabotaging their careers.

What High-Performing Organizations Can Do

As an organization, you are accountable for creating your culture. Articulating expectations for your employees and holding them accountable is a must in order to shift away from micro-aggressions and into a productive and more inclusive, high-performing culture. These expectations should become part of every job description and year-end review process so that each and every employee and leader is held to the same high-performance standard.

Written and expressed workplace expectations should not only contain actions that can be used to stop pervasive and micro-aggressions but should also contain examples of positive behavior. This will create a workforce that feels valued, respected, and can bring their best every day. In addition, everyone in the workplace will be happier and more productive.

Here are a few of the expectations you can communicate around micro-aggressions:

> **Exclusion** – Expectation: Inclusive meetings. When establishing meetings, think through the different perspectives you need to have in order to accomplish your goal. Seek out women and high performers in your organization who will provide a unique

way of thinking or who have a different perspective that would benefit the group. Set everyone up for success by articulating the lens through which you would like them to participate. High-performing teams value different perspectives, including the ability to think through downstream impact.

Dismissing – Expectation: Give credit for original ideas. Try to keep track of where the original idea generated from and give credit where credit is due. Don't allow recency bias – giving credit to the last one to talk or the loudest voice – to creep in. Encourage reaffirming behavior in meetings, including a simple nod, smile, or relaxed eye contact when anyone is speaking.

Talking over – Expectation: Everyone gets to finish their thought. This is easy to stop, as no one should interrupt another person. If a team member experiences this in a meeting, they should stop the interrupter and ask the speaker to finish.

Challenging women and high performers – Expectation: The three-question rule. If someone begins drilling someone else with a line of questions, they should be held accountable to limit these to the best questions. Overquestioning can quickly turn into bullying in the workplace. If it occurs in a meeting, others should be able to step in, offering explanations of what they are hearing, providing their insight, then asking the speaker to elaborate on the topic at hand. This blocks the aggressive behavior and puts the power back in the hands of the original speaker, allowing them time to think and respond from a position of strength. It also puts the questioner on notice.

Micro-Aggression	High-Performance Behaviors
Exclusion	Inclusive meetings
Dismissing	Giving credit for ideas
Talking over speakers	Allowing speakers to finish
Challenging speakers with overquestioning	Limiting to three top questions

Reinforce Positive High-Performing Behaviors

Fortunately, there are positive cultural traits called micro-affirmations and micro-advantages, and these are small but powerful behavior boosts that can counter the negative work of micro-aggressions.

Micro-affirmations are essentially the exact opposite of pervasive and micro-aggressions. They are small but powerful infusions of energy into the workplace, a universal language and widely recognized actions of respect.

Here are some examples of how executives, leaders, and peers can shift the workplace to high performance, especially for their top talent and women who have faced barriers for years:

> **Micro-affirmations** are small ways of showing respect for a person's value and accomplishments, helping them feel part of a group. These can include simple signs of basic respect: opening a door for someone, smiling and saying hi in the hallway, or acknowledging something they did well.
>
> **Micro-advantages** are gestures, facial expressions, choices of words, and tones that are even *more* subtle but just as important in making a person feel valued and appreciated. Examples of micro-advantages are making eye contact, nodding and smiling, and not crossing your arms.

Eliminating pervasive aggressions and micro-inequities and introducing new rules in your workplace will have a host of positive effects on your employees and leaders and help you design a high-performing workforce:

> **Higher employee engagement**. Work units in the top quartile in employee engagement outperformed bottom-quartile units by 10% on customer ratings, 22% in profitability, and 21% in productivity. Work units in the top quartile also saw significantly lower turnover (25% in high-turnover organizations, 65% in

low-turnover organizations), lower rates of inventory theft or loss (28%), less absenteeism (37%), and fewer safety incidents (48%), patient safety incidents (41%), and quality defects (41%).[2] The following chart from Gallup shows just how dramatic these gains are for high-performing organizations.

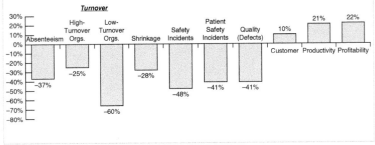

EMPLOYEE ENGAGEMENT AFFECTS KEY BUSINESS OUTCOMES

Work units in the top quartile in employee engagement outperform bottom-quartile units by 10% on customer ratings, 21% in productivity, and 22% in profitability. Work units in the tap quartile also saw significantly lower absenteeism (37%), turnover (25% in high-turnover organizations, 65% in low-turnover organizations), and shrinkage (28%) and fewer safety incidents (48%), patient safety incidents (41%), and quality defects (41%).

Source: GALLUP

In fact, a company seeking to increase employee engagement can make immediate gains by promoting more women to the ranks of management and, especially, by pairing them with female team members to lead and mentor. According to Gallup's employee engagement studies, "Female managers are more likely to be engaged than male managers (41% to 35%, respectively). Individuals who work for a female manager are also six percentage points more engaged, on average, than those who work for a male manager.

---

[2]Sorenson, Susan, "Employee Engagement Drives Growth," Gallup, June 20, 2013. https://www.gallup.com/workplace/236927/employee-engagement-drives-growth.aspx.

"Female employees working for female managers have the highest engagement (35% engaged), while male employees working for male managers have the lowest engagement (25% engaged)."[3] That isn't to say that male managers and employees can't be high performers. Rather, a company that fails to empower and engage female managers is missing an opportunity for a valuable contribution to its productivity and overall effectiveness.

Less turnover. All of your employees, particularly women, will be less inclined to think about leaving a company when they are in a positive and encouraging environment where the rules are the same for everyone and are followed by leadership. This sets companies on a more positive trajectory of employee retention, higher engagement, and superior performance.

Greater impact and results. When a person is more positively motivated at work, they can think clearly and are more innovative and solution-oriented versus spending their time and energy on how to play the corporate political game. Employees who are highly engaged work with passion and feel a profound connection to their jobs. They view their jobs as energizing and rewarding, and they like where and how they spend their days.

In a high-performing company, Taylor's story would have played out very differently:

While Taylor is sitting at her cubicle, Zack, one of her colleagues, walks by, stops to say hello, and asks how she's doing. They have small talk and then Zack makes his way to Corey's cube. Corey says hi to Zach and asks if he has any great ideas for the get-together on Sunday. Zach says he and Taylor were just talking about it yesterday and she thought that it might be fun to meet at the local brewery for dinner. Taylor adds that she was there a few weeks ago for dinner and the cuisine was really good, with enough variety that

---

[3] Adkins, Amy. "Report: What Separates Great Managers From the Rest," Gallup, May 12, 2015, https://www.gallup.com/workplace/236594/report-separates-great-managers-rest.aspx.

everyone should find something they like. Corey said he thinks it sounds great and he'll let everyone know about Taylor's idea.

Taylor walks into her next meeting with some of the key managers: Anthony, Jim, Mike, and Doug, all from her division. Taylor is there, along with her co-lead, Alex, to provide a project overview and status, as well as to request approval to move forward.

Anthony, the leader, kicks off the meeting by stating that they are there to hear from Taylor and Alex, who will present their project update and are requesting to move forward with the project. He would like the team to help them identify any risks or benefits. At the end of the meeting the team will make a decision on next steps. He welcomes Taylor and Alex and lets them know that the leadership team is excited to hear their thoughts.

Taylor thanks Anthony and kicks off the meeting by stating that they researched the original direction, but that she and Alex think that there is a more cost-effective way to accomplish their goals with an even greater result. Alex jumps in and supports the statement, saying that he and Taylor really gave this some thought, and he is excited about their proposal.

Taylor picks up where Alex leaves off, continuing to propose and explain their rationale. As Taylor talks, Jim talks over her and asks Alex a question. Anthony stops Jim and states that he would like to hear what Taylor has to say and asks that he let her finish. Jim agrees and apologizes to Taylor. When she is finished, Anthony asks Jim if he has any questions. He does – five, in fact. Anthony asks him to limit them to his top three. As Taylor answers Jim's questions, Doug stares at her in an intimidating way. Anthony notices the aggressive behavior and asks Doug if there is an issue, as he notices that he is listening very intently. Doug says no and stops the intimidating play. Taylor and Alex tag team the questions and answers and support each other with additional information if needed.

Doug closes his eyes, folds his arms, and puts his chin on his chest as if he is taking a quick nap. After a few minutes, Anthony stops the meeting and asks Doug a question to reengage him. Doug shrugs his shoulders and has a limited response.

Anthony then asks the team if they need any additional information to be able to make a decision. At this point, Doug starts to respond to e-mails on his phone. The other leaders stated that they had all the information they need and that they would like to move forward with Taylor and Alex's proposal. Doug remains silent. Anthony then asks Doug for his decision. He states he is fine with that direction.

Anthony compliments Taylor and Zach on their ideas, preparedness, and courage to think differently. Taylor and Zach leave the meeting ecstatic and highly engaged.

After the meeting, Anthony asks Doug to stay behind. He shares with Doug that the reason he was invited to the meeting was because he was looking forward to his perspective. However, his behavior proved otherwise. Anthony tells Doug that he noticed him aggressively staring at Taylor, and that he was largely disengaged during the meeting but when he did engage, had a lot of questions. He asks if there is an issue he would like to discuss. Doug appears startled and embarrassed that he is being called out. He says no, he was fine. Anthony also shares that his aggressive staring, coupled with his disconnection during the meeting, could be perceived as an aggressive play on Taylor, which would be inappropriate and against the company leadership code. He just wants to let him know so he can be aware in the future. Doug thanks Anthony and leaves the meeting room. If Anthony needs Doug's perspective in the future, he will invite Doug's boss instead.

High-performing organizations need more leaders like Anthony.

5 | Removing Bad Bosses Who Under-Promote Women and High Performers

"75% of workers who voluntarily changed jobs did so because of their bosses, not the job itself."[1]

Bosses play a critical role in the careers of their employees. The great ones invest in their teams, assign challenging projects that maximize and align to their talent, provide timely feedback, and truly care about their success. They are also strategic, respected among their peer group and executive team, and collaborate effectively across the organization and industry. Bosses motivate those around them to come to work each day, inspiring them to be incredibly loyal, and create an environment where everyone wants the best for the company.

---

[1] Hyacinth, Brigette, "Employees Don't Leave Companies, They Leave Managers," LinkedIn, December 27, 2017, https://www.linkedin.com/pulse/employees-dont-leave-companies-managers-brigette-hyacinth.

Unfortunately, according to the statistics, the reality is that most bosses are at best mediocre; in fact, anywhere between 30% and 60% of workers consider their boss to be somewhere between bad and toxic. That's not a good track record of leadership. It also means that an employee should plan on having more bad bosses than good ones. Bad bosses are one of the main reasons employees leave their jobs because they tend to cause feelings of powerlessness, ask co-workers to tackle tasks beneath their impact or talent level, and, even worse, constantly berate their subordinates and create an environment of fear within the organization. If leadership fails to address bad bosses, they can undermine high performers viewed as a threat to their power and position, while bullying or intimidating female colleagues for any number of reasons.

Women and high performers, particularly those early in their careers, tend to look to their boss as their main (and sometimes only) advocate, so bosses become critical to their success. This can also be true for mid- or late-career women and high performers who are new to an organization and typically do not have a well-established network.

The good news? These are typically acute situations, which means they are short-lived.

The bad news? The situations that arise under a bad boss have a memorable impact.

According to Lean In's 2019 Women in the Workplace Report, a woman's first promotion to manager is the biggest obstacle in her career. They call for companies to fix this "broken rung," and having a great boss is critical to making that happen.[2]

The key to managing a bad boss is first to determine what type of bad boss they are so they can be identified. Then leaders

---

[2]"Women in the Workplace," McKinsey & Company and LeanIn.Org, 2019.

can put this bad boss on a development plan, limit this person's impact on women and high performers, or remove them from the organization completely. For women and high performers, it is also critical to understand the tactics of a bad boss in order to decide how best to professionally address the inequity.

Following are some examples of the different types of bad bosses who impede talent in an organization.

The Miserable Boss

Devon graduated with honors after working two jobs to pay her way through college. In her first job out of college, she had "that" manager – the manager she would never want to be. This manager, named Alicia, berated Devon in front of her team, only provided critical feedback, and even made inappropriate comments about her clothing ("It's not Friday yet, you aren't going to find a man here."). It was a nightmare situation.

Little did Devon know that Alicia was dealing with a situation of her own. Alicia also wanted to get promoted, but she too had a bad boss – Maureen. Maureen was rarely available to give direction or take questions, but if Alicia made a decision without feedback, Maureen would call, yelling at her for making "stupid" decisions. Alicia had complained to HR, but they said they were "working through the issues." No help for her, either. So, Alicia continued to work 70 hours a week, doing both her job and Maureen's job, which is why she treated Devon so poorly. Devon and Alicia were both miserable because of a bad boss and might have worked together effectively if they had had better leadership.

Higher-level bad bosses permeate the organization, causing negative impact through their direct reports to the team. Great bosses have the opposite effect, infusing engagement through – and to – the masses.

The Powerless Boss

Rachel landed a dream job at a top-tier company after graduating from college. She seemed to have it all. In college, everyone liked her; she was smart, driven, a great leader, and had plans to be successful.

During her first year at work, Rachel worked 70 hours per week and learned her role inside and out. She received additional responsibilities and felt that she was headed in the right direction. And then she got passed over for that coveted first promotion; James got the job instead.

Her boss had told her that she had a good chance of getting it, but when it didn't happen, she became frustrated, especially because she knew she would do a better job than James. Her boss told Rachel to try again in six months. Six months felt like a really long time to keep working those long hours. Should she look for another job? Why did James get the job and not her?

But no matter how many questions she asked, her manager offered little to no perspective.

"Just keep doing what you're doing," her boss repeated.

Powerless bosses can be smart, talented, and good people, but they lack the impact to convince or persuade others during a promotion meeting. These are good bosses because you feel cared for and appreciated, yet they lack the ability to provide you with a career path or visibility. And when it is time to advocate for your next promotion or a highly visible project, they fall short. Their peers typically describe them as nice but may snicker behind their back.

Powerless bosses should not be responsible for leading people and here's why: it is critical for women and high performers to have an advocate at the promotion table. If they do not, the loudest voice of an imposter leader overshadows the conversations, promoting their underlings into leadership positions. At promotion time, great leaders advocate for their top performers, including the women, on their team, thus putting real, high-performing leaders into critical positions.

The New Boss

Rebecca worked at her company for over five years and had been promoted multiple times. She was ready for a director-level job. Her boss of the last three years shifted to another department, so she started reporting to a new, inexperienced boss from the outside who had never led a department before. He was cocky, smart, driven, and ready to make change happen.

Rebecca had just spent the last two years making the changes her prior boss had wanted, but this new boss had an entirely different management style. He was very aggressive. He wanted things immediately, without fully considering their risks and impacts. Rebecca knew the department, the people, the history, and had a lot to offer, but although she spoke up on numerous occasions, her new boss ignored her insight.

During her one-on-one meetings with him, she shared her department plan and how it would positively impact the overall company goals. He approved but never truly engaged with her or her department. After six months, he started dropping hints that there could be organizational changes that might affect her role. When she asked for specifics, he just said that the changes could happen in three to six months. When she asked how her plans might need to change to accommodate his direction, he would not answer her. He was giving her the Heisman.

In four months, he unveiled his new reorganization and Rebecca no longer had a role on his team. She was replaced by Joe, his friend and buddy from his previous organization. Rebecca was not only out of a job, but she was no longer going to work for a company where she had spent years cultivating a reputation and connections.

New leaders of an organization who need the security blanket of a previous team or team member, especially if they remove a current woman or high performer from your company, put everyone on notice, losing engagement and loyalty and illuminating your weak performance infrastructure. Great leaders don't need to feel secure or protected. They are the ones creating security and protection for their high performers, women, and teams.

The Absent Boss

Will had finally received a promotion to manager. It was a role he had worked years to achieve. He had a great leader who provided him opportunity, feedback, and clearly outlined expectations at all times. At the same time Will was promoted, so was his boss, moving her into a higher level within the organization. Will's new boss had been in the organization a long time and was looking forward to retirement. His days were spent on the golf course, tending to building his new home in another state, and traveling. This left little time to run his large business line/department. When Will attempted to set up time to clarify expectations or to propose a new program that would create operational efficiency, his boss would respond days later, setting up time the next week. When the date arrived for the meeting, the new boss would reschedule for an even later date. Will was a high performer, ready to learn, to lead his expanded team, and to make a positive impact in the organization. Having no direction, few expectations, and no insight into the goals of the organization hampered his ability.

Absent bosses fill their schedules with meetings (on site and off), cancel your one-on-ones (if you even manage to schedule them in the first place), and are concerned only with themselves and their own careers. Their team (including you) is simply a means to an end for them. These bosses may say all of the right things (i.e., I care about you or you are a really good performer or I need you on this team), but that is only to pacify you so that you don't leave and create disruption in their lives.

Absent bosses cause an immense amount of frustration because their lack of availability directly impacts the ability of those around them to adequately perform their jobs and to receive the support they need to advance their careers.

Staying too long in a company or position simply to get a paycheck stalls progress in your organization. Great leaders set the career goal to finish strong and to retire on top of their game.

The Incompetent Boss

Early in her career, Monique had hit her stride. She was leading her team to success, identifying top talent that was promoted, sometimes higher than herself. She was a go-to for others in the organization – offering sage advice as a trustworthy mentor. Monique was also on the high-potential list and was working toward her next promotion to senior director when she began reporting to a new boss, Maria. Maria was known throughout the organization as someone who was not the sharpest tool in the shed but had built a reputation for getting the job done. She was very good at leveraging others' knowledge and expertise to create plans and then execute them, taking the credit for everything that went well. The most frustrating part about working for Maria was that her knowledge was an inch deep and a mile wide. She never tried to really learn about the department she was leading or was truly interested in learning about its people strengths. She used people's skills and organized them, but she had little to no knowledge herself. When the experts on her team would require guidance or insight, she would refer them to others in the organization, acting as if it was a "learning opportunity." Sometimes a decision she did weigh in on would set the team in the wrong direction, wasting countless hours of time, and then she would blame the team for the decision.

When employees complain about their boss, incompetence is usually the number-one issue. These bosses can be a little more dangerous than others because they think they know what they are doing but really don't. They will ask you to perform duties that make no sense, will value your performance on characteristics that have little to do with your role (but value what they know), and are ineffective at coaching you to perform at your highest ability. You will feel stuck and have no idea what direction you are your career is going. Everything will feel like it's on hold, or, worse yet, moving in the wrong direction.

These bosses can be difficult to gauge, and they often hide their lack of ability with enthusiasm or rash action. They may also turn key decisions back to you, so they can blame you later. Be aware of this when a new boss arrives on the scene, and don't be enamored with their over-the-top positive communication or ability to relate with the team.

Incompetence is the most pervasive "bad boss" in corporate America today. Incompetent individuals are dangerous for your organization because they do not identify or promote the most competent or high performers, but rather those who have the skills they are lacking and who are most loyal to them. Great leaders are highly competent, aggressive learners who are consistently applying what they've learned to advance their people and the organization.

The Power Seat Boss

Tyler had reported to his boss for over five years, and his strategy up to this point was to simply avoid him at all costs. If he had to communicate or engage with him, it was more than likely not going to be a good situation. Tyler's boss, Cary, was known throughout the organization as a tyrant. Unfortunately for everyone, he was also the CFO's best friend, so no one would ever report his abusive behavior. Nothing would be done about it anyway.

Cary would come onto the shop floor, and yell at someone inches from their face. His main objective was to embarrass you, ridicule you, or get you to quit, especially if he didn't like you. He would expect jobs to be done in half the regular time but charge his customer the full price, thus making his department's bottom line look better. Some compared Cary's use of fear and unreasonable demands to working in a sweat shop. One day, he came onto the floor and started questioning one of the new guys. Most of the questions were rhetorical in nature to make the employee look bad. Cary yelled, his arms flying all around him. He used his height as power and dominance over others. Sometimes he would just come out into the shop to create an issue where none existed, making everyone wonder if all was right with him. When it was time for the annual "employee survey," people would just mark that all was okay because they feared what would happen if they said otherwise, so the abusive behavior continued and nothing was done.

The issue with a power seat boss is that they gain power by taking away from others, strictly for their own self-gratification. This can be done in public (as with Tyler) or in private, where the boss can intellectually outmaneuver their target. Their feedback is typically given inappropriately and is questionable but because they are in a power seat, the employee has to take it and do what they say. The target will feel an even greater wrath if they question the power seat boss in public or private. This only fuels the fire and they may find a different path to punish the target.

These individuals could be thought of highly by senior management because they are experts at managing up or appeasing the people they report to. Employee survey results could be positive because the employees are reluctant to tell the truth either for fear of retaliation or because, based upon prior history, they feel that their cry for help will be ignored.

Protecting bad bosses because of nepotism or personal relationships impedes productivity and engagement and ultimately will ensure that top performers and women leave your organization. Great leaders only expect the best from their teams, regardless of whether they are family or a close personal friend.

The Unethical Boss

Karen had built a reputation as a high-performing leader. She was smart, driven, and ethical, and was a great leader of people. When she committed to a project or individual, she always followed through. Unfortunately, a new boss was hired into the company from the outside and Karen had to begin reporting to her. At first, the new boss was fun, engaging, and supportive, constantly asking for Karen's opinion and about how things were done in the past. She even gave Karen a raise, stating that she was at the bottom of her range for the job she was doing. Although Karen had received top raises and bonuses, she had never received a pay adjustment off the typical company schedule. Karen soon became a close confidant of her new leader.

One day, the leader approached Karen with a list of everyone in the department and put a star next to a team member's name. She said the star meant the person had to go. She didn't like her and was no longer "welcome" in her department. This team member had been with the company almost 30 years, was a steady performer, always had a great attitude, and would take on additional work or help others as needed. She also had a stellar work history and ratings.

The following week, it was budget time and there was a lot of money left in the budget that wasn't spent due to significant efficiency gains that were implemented before the new leader arrived. The new leader asked Karen to change the numbers to wipe out the savings. Karen had already had a sleepless week because of the pressure to fire a perfectly good employee and now her new boss was telling her to do something completely illegal! She later scheduled a meeting with her new boss and stated that she would not fire the employee nor would she change the numbers. Both requests were unethical and illegal and she would not play a role in either. The new boss became irate and told her if she didn't do it, she would fire Karen. Karen was later fired for not complying with her boss's demands.

The unethical boss will strain every part of your belief system and amplify your fear. They will lie about you, cheat the business, and put the organization in questionable situations. But beware! When you attempt to address or expose them, they will wage an all-out war to discredit you. The good news is that eventually they are exposed and their power stripped (although you may be a short-term casualty). The bad news is that it could take years.

These people are typically very driven and will do anything to get where they want to go. They have no moral compass and will lie, cheat, and steal to achieve their goals. Some are very afraid – of failure and of success. They are a deathtrap to anyone working for them, unless you are equally as unethical as they are.

Of all the bad bosses on this list, unethical ones will often create the worst of situations, particularly if you have a strong sense of right and wrong and want to do good in the workplace and world.

Unethical bosses are a sign of the lack of performance infrastructure and accountability in an organization, especially of your leaders. These bad bosses will cause irreparable damage to your organization, brand, and people, causing confusion over what is truly right and wrong in your organization. Great bosses never tolerate unethical practices; in fact, engaging in them is grounds for immediate termination.

When a Low-Performing Culture Sets the Tone for Bosses

Bad bosses thrive in low-performing organizations because it feeds their desire for power without the accountability of performing. When a boss, either a man or woman, runs their department based on culturally low-performing characteristics, risks are especially multiplied among women and high performers in the workplace. Why? Because combining a bad boss and a low-performing infrastructure leads to the worst possible outcomes no matter how exceptional their talent or leadership.

Here's why:

When it comes to hiring, bad bosses are always on the lookout for others with their same qualities – most managers hire people just like them. It's difficult for a bad boss to understand or appreciate the value high performers bring to the table. A bad male boss may see women as inferior workers, while a bad female boss may see capable women as a threat to the limited number of positions open to women in the company. Many of these types of managers think women and high performers possess only "soft skills," which results in their contributions being minimized and overlooked.

If a woman and/or high performer is able to initially succeed but is placed on a team with a bad boss with low-performance characteristics, they are much more likely to fail. Aggressive, political tactics and low-performing models of feedback present serious barriers for employees with potential to grow and make a positive impact in your organization.

Beyond those issues, the feedback offered by an imposter boss is often questionable. Bad bosses in a low-performing culture are especially uncomfortable giving women and high performers feedback – some fear that women will cry or a particularly sharp subordinate will debate them. In order to avoid such situations, imposter bosses avoid giving valuable feedback. Or the feedback they give is based solely on low-performing traits and culture, which are contrary to the diverse, natural approaches and talents of the high-performing men and women in their company.

Women and high performers may be able to initially navigate a low-performing company and even an imposter boss, but their ability to receive consistent promotions is limited because these bosses rarely promote anyone who is unlike them. Imposter bosses view any signs of inquisitiveness as a direct challenge to their authority and position.

Do you know the reality in corporate America today?

Most women and high performers work under imposter bosses, and most employees report that their bosses are toxic, both of which are reasons that a majority of women and high performers have a harder time making it through the talent pipeline and occupying critical roles in corporate America.

What Women and High Performers Can Do

The first step in dealing with a bad boss is knowing how to identify one so that you can respond appropriately to their behavior.

While in the middle of a situation with a bad boss, it can be difficult to keep perspective. For those caught up in a low-performing culture, this is especially difficult. Always remember this: how an individual handles the situation is a choice. It should always be your goal to show the best of who you are, even if the other person is showing the worst of who they are.

As Glinda the Good Witch said to Dorothy, "You have always had the power, my dear. You just needed to use it."

There are three primary approaches when dealing with a bad boss: (1) Accept what's going on and try to wait them out. (2) Work hard to try to improve the relationship and situation.

Or (3) Fire them.

Fire them?

I'll get into that in a second.

First, let's look at option number one: Wait them out and hope they get fired or move on. When deciding to wait it out, start by getting a clear view of the situation by asking others for perspective. For example, talk to other people who have worked for this bad boss (but always in a positive tone). "You successfully worked for Kevin. Can you help me understand his approach and what worked with him?" This might give a better understanding into Kevin's values, what he actually expects, and how others handled the outcomes that came with working for him.

Another option while waiting it out includes talking to a mentor. Approach a mentor in the same positive way. When sharing any stories, stick to the facts and try to avoid getting into feelings or sharing other options you're considering. This is simply an information-gathering mission, with the goal of figuring out how to work effectively with this person.

By now you should have some valuable information about how your boss works, what they expect, and the kind of experiences others have had with them. The final thing you want to consider before making any long-term decisions is to take into account the fluidity of the boss's role. Do managers in that position move around frequently, or has your boss held that position for years and years? Do you suspect your boss is vying for another job or an upcoming promotion?

What you are trying to figure out with these questions is whether you love your job enough to tolerate a bad boss for a period of time.

Let's assume that after you think through these things and gather as much information as you can, you decide to stay and do your best to improve the situation. If that's where you land, it's important that you do a few things.

First, write down specifically what you are and are not willing to tolerate, without compromising your character, ethics, or integrity. If there's any illegal action taking place, always seek an attorney for advice on how to handle the situation.

Once you've written out what you're willing to tolerate, begin working steadily to improve the situation. Depending upon the issue at hand, some imposter bosses don't even realize the impact they are having on others. It is a risk, but you can attempt to mitigate the issues by having a conversation with them. Sometimes your boss is stuck or finds themselves in a bad situation. If you can help them, do so, but never compromise your ethics or integrity. Your company typically has an appropriate way to engage in conflict, so ask your human resources person for advice if you think this kind of conversation could lead to heated exchanges. The goal of this kind of meeting is always to make sure your expectations of each other are in writing and are clear. Always follow up by sending them an e-mail recapping your conversation.

In the meantime, expand your network so that others are aware of your contributions. One way to do this is by establishing a network of mentors. Each mentor should exhibit key qualities you share or want to improve in yourself. Your time should be spent learning from them just as much as you want them to be aware of your most-prized contributions. There should be a healthy mix of women and men from inside your company, industry, and other industries.

As you continue working with a bad boss, you might begin to notice signs of micro-aggressions, bullying, or abuse. If that's the case, you might want to set up a meeting with HR and ask them what is appropriate at your workplace and what is not. What is a fireable offense and what is considered coachable? Always remember, HR works for the company, not for you. Their primary interest is in de-escalating situations so they do not turn into a legal actions. To do so, they will support and side with their leaders. HR is *not* your support system. Only an external mentor, family member, or lawyer can truly help you advocate for your situation. It's important to understand the approach of your HR department, their views of certain behaviors, and where your boss falls in their spectrum of fireable offenses.

As you move forward, keep a journal and document each day, including what happened, what was said, and the time, location, and identities of others in the room. This will not only be your best insurance policy if your boss wants to fire you, but will provide you daily, weekly, and monthly perspective as you look back on the situation.

If none of this helps you get through the pain of having an imposter boss, and if the situation continues to deteriorate no matter how much effort you put into it, you'll need to move on to your final option.

Fire them.

And by that, I mean firing them by starting the process of finding another job. At a minimum, a job search provides you with an element of security in case the imposter boss eliminates your role or heads down the path of performance management. The best-case scenario is that you interview and gain back some confidence or, even better, are offered another job with a great boss.

Keep in mind that you work at your current job because a boss made a decision to hire you and you made a decision to accept. Either one of you can fire the other at any time.

Consider it a possible push in the right direction!

★★★★★

These situations can be difficult and they can take a toll on the rest of your life. Try to remember that a situation like this is temporary – it will not last forever and you will get a new boss. It may take months or even a few years, but the change will happen because either you will leave or the boss will leave. It's that simple.

It is your choice to determine how long you are willing to stay in the situation, so figure out your game plan. Some women and high performers resist the change because they feel strongly that the bad bosses are the ones who should be forced to leave, but in over 60% of the cases, the person who is being bullied moves on because HR will categorize these situations as a "personality conflict" to reduce their own legal risk.

Don't let them define what you are dealing with.

For you, it is critical that you remain empowered throughout the process. And when you do, you will feel ready to take on your next challenge!

What Leaders Can Do

Today's corporate low-performance culture dictates that leaders who witness or learn about a negative interaction between a bad boss and talented employees recuse themselves. Perhaps they'll at most offer sage advice. Either way, these leaders send employees on their way to battle the lion alone.

If we truly want to shift the culture so that women and high performers succeed in corporate America, leaders need to do more.

First, as a leader of an organization, you are responsible for creating the culture – a culture that inspires and motivates *every* employee in the company. Take an inventory of the women and high performers you know and whether they report to a bad boss. If the results show that more than 20% of your women and high performers report to a bad boss, you should advocate for substantive leadership development efforts within your organization, including rewriting the leadership expectations in your performance management system.

Secondly, you must make an effort to mentor women and high performers or introduce them to someone who can offer advice through their journey with the bad boss. Supporting women and high performers through these critical times is imperative if your organization wants to keep top talent.

Third, every leader should be required to make mandatory reports on any bad boss situation if it is hindering the progress of talent in your organization, especially if there is bullying or any type of abusive situation.

Finally, and most importantly, advocate for women and high performers to be moved to a different boss during performance management discussions, especially if you believe they are under-utilized. Again, it is your job to manage corporate resources, and by advocating for employees, you are doing just that.

What Organizations Can Do

Ask anyone to describe their best boss and you will likely hear common traits.

"They were supportive."

"They challenged me to grow."

"They identified talents in me I never knew I had."

"Under their leadership, I accomplished more in my role than I ever thought possible."

Great leaders inspire teams to perform at their very best. The best bosses identify strengths and align them to initiatives where their team members can shine and accomplish more than anyone thought possible. They are fair, honest, and provide immediate feedback.

The role of organizations, executive teams, and human resource departments is maximizing each person's performance in the organization. Aligning women and high performers with the right boss is critical for the health of the organization *as well as* being critical to their personal success. There are a few things organizations can do to encourage these outcomes, and HR will be critical in creating the path and processes needed to remove and replace the bad boss barrier.

First, place women and high performers with bosses who are exhibiting the new high-performance expectations and who have the courage to both develop and protect them. These leaders should be known for developing their people into high performers who can impact other parts of the business. Aligning women and high performers with great leaders establishes a strong foundation of skills for your organization. This puts your best talent in a position to become great leaders themselves and to lead their teams with increased engagement, impact, and results.

If you want a high-performing culture to succeed and to spread, mentors are also critical. Create thoughtfully aligned mentoring roles for the women and high performers in your organization. Women and high performers need support from others within your organization to succeed. If you cannot align the women and high performers to report directly to a best boss, align them to best bosses in a mentor/mentee relationship.

Next, develop a team within HR that offers career coaching and insight based upon the new high-performance expectations. As the experts within your organization, you would be able to provide hands-on, practical, real-time advice that aligns with your culture, thus creating the shift to high performance as you identify and address the imposter bosses in your organization while keeping your top talent engaged. Studies and surveys have consistently found that a more engaged workforce performs significantly better across a wide range of categories.[3]

Engagement's Effect on Key Business Outcomes

When compared with business units in the bottom quartile of engagement, those in the top quartile realize improvements in the following areas:

GALLUP

Your success is in the numbers because what gets measured gets done. Develop and implement employee engagement and retention goals for the women and high performers in your organization. The Gallup Workplace Engagement Survey is a great place to start and will also help you identify whether women and high performers are

---

[3]Reilly, Robin. "5 Ways to Improve Employee Engagement Now," Gallup. January 7, 2014, https://www.gallup.com/workplace/231581/five-ways-improve-employee-engagement.aspx.

receiving the development and support they need to be successful (consequentially, this survey will also help you identify your best and worst bosses). It will also help you identify and promote your best bosses to replace those existing bad bosses.

Aligning women and high performers with great bosses is critical for their own development, impact, and performance. It establishes a strong connection and example of what a great boss truly is in your organization based upon objective, external measures (such as the Gallup Workplace Engagement Survey). If you want to retain your most talented employees, these practices are a must and HR is critical to making the shift in leadership from bad bosses to great ones.

However, dealing with bad bosses won't bring about the shift your company needs in order to be competitive in the long term. You also need to make sure bad bosses don't accumulate power and influence in the first place. Shifting to a high-performing workplace requires an overhaul of the dysfunctional promotion system.

6

Removing the Promotion Dysfunction

"Companies fail to make the right person manager 82% of the time."
Gallup[1]

Remember the story about Bella in Chapter 3? She entered the workforce as a college graduate and was more qualified than any of her peers, but because she didn't have the same rapport with the trainer as the men, she was appointed an average manager and overlooked for early promotion. This is a good time to address women and true high-performing men in the workplace. Although corporations are hiring more women out of college, men are not only hired to a greater degree, but receive their first promotion at a much

---

[1]Beck, Randall, and Jim Harter, "Managers Account for 70% of Employee Variance," Gallup, April 21, 2015, https://news.gallup.com/businessjournal/182792/managers-account-variance-employee-engagement.aspx.

higher rate than women. That is not a slight against men, but rather a reflection of the flawed hiring and promotion ecosystem in many organizations that often leads directly to low performance.

This is where women are introduced to the low-performance culture for the first time in the workplace, and it can be shocking and confusing. It can even turn them off from their chosen field.

Women think, *Shouldn't my work speak for itself?*

Yes, it should.

Encouraging women to lean in and to stay in the game can work out, and it's certainly a necessary message because of all the dysfunctional workplaces and bosses in the world.

But there is another approach that is equally as important: a method that companies can use to stop the inequity from the very beginning, from the first days of a talented employee's career.

To make the shift from encouraging women and high performers through a difficult system to changing the system entirely, we need to acknowledge what is happening in the workplace and what needs to happen to create a high-performing workplace where women *and the right men* can thrive. For example, low-performance cultures tell overlooked women, "Your career is a marathon, not a sprint. Just because someone gets promoted early on in their career does not mean it will continue. There are different requirements at each level and therefore each promotion. Hang in there, your time will come."

While this may be true at times, there are only a few who persevere and stick it out in such workplaces. Even if they do stick it out, the vast majority are not engaged in their work – which may in part be linked to the broken promotion system at many workplaces. In fact, only 30% of American workers are engaged with their jobs, and that percentage has hardly budged over the years.[2]

---

[2]Sorenson, Susan, and Keri Garman, "How to Tackle US Employees' Stagnating Engagement," Gallup, June 11, 2013. https://news.gallup

Only Three in 10 American Workers Are Engaged

Employee engagement remains stagnant among U.S. workers, according to Gallup's State of the American Workplace: 2010–2012 report. Only about three in 10 American workers are engaged. Meanwhile, an overwhelming seven in 10 are not showing up to work committed to delivering their best performance. This has serious implications for the bottom line of individual companies and for the U.S. economy.

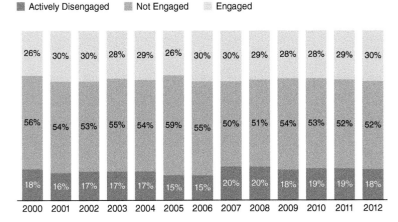

GALLUP

We've come to realize that when women are outpromoted from the very beginning of their career, it is hard to catch up over time. It's even easier to give up.

Why should women continue to play a game they cannot win? They become disillusioned and defeated because the game is either not clearly defined or it's rigged against them.

For men, most often the overly competitive, assertive, and sometimes aggressive of them are the ones who are identified for the first promotion because they are viewed as someone who is going to drive the business forward. Little consideration is given to whether he is a great leader of people – let alone a high performer.

.com/businessjournal/162953/tackle-employees-stagnating-engagement
.aspx.

As result, women are held back, and men rise to leadership positions based on false positive traits or traits from a leader in a bygone era.

The sole accountability for change in the workplace should be directed at the executive team, HR, and leadership, not the women or the overlooked high-performing men.

What Women and High Performers Can Do

We've talked about what leaders can do in order to promote the best talent within an organization, but where does this leave overlooked but high-performing men and women?

If you're waiting on a "delayed" promotion, I can help you make the most of your opportunities. If you're a leader or executive in charge of promotions, the following list will help you identify the right kind of talent to promote. Here are a few tips to be the star performer you were meant to be in order to get that promotion you deserve:

1. Do the absolute best you can at every job, using the talents you have while getting the job done. Be a great leader, peer, and executive go-to.
2. Proactively receive clarity about what success looks like in your current role and the next level above you. Set your goal for a promotion and ask your leader to help you identify what it will take to achieve it. You must have a clear idea of what success looks like at the next level to get the promotion. What experiences do you need? What impact should you make in your current role? Then ask your mentor the same questions to gain insight from more than one person around the decision table.
3. If you are invited to meet with another manager, be prepared to talk about your career aspirations, agreed-upon goals developed with your manager, what you feel good about thus far, and where you could use their feedback or support. Also use

the time to ask about their success. There are gold nuggets to be found in stories about leaders who have succeeded in your organization. Be open to any and all feedback (what you do with it is your decision), and always thank them for their time, both formally and informally.

4. Stay in the game. Do not let the lack of early promotion keep you from your dream or your rightful place as a leader at an organization. Keep believing in yourself. You – and only you – know what you are capable of. You may not experience the success you deserve at this particular company, but you will achieve it someday. Everything will happen at the right time for you.

5. If you do not get promoted, strive to ensure that your manager is candid and upfront as to the reason why. If they begin to hide or are not forthcoming, this is a red flag. Trust your gut in these situations.

6. If you do not get promoted and others do, there are many reasons you will not be privy to. This is not necessarily a red flag (e.g., the position required more technical expertise than you have at the moment, etc.). Again, the key is to have an open and candid dialogue with your manager or mentor.

7. Be prepared for candor. If the feedback you receive is legit (in other words, given with the best of intentions and coupled with truth) and there is a gap in your performance, you have some questions to consider: Can you either acquire the skills or do you have the talent to close the gap? If so, focus on making the required changes. But if you believe the feedback is ill-placed or not true, this is definitely not the person you want to report to, and this company may not be the place you want to work. Think through the options we talked about earlier in the chapter, and begin planning a new path forward.

8. In all situations, remain in full control. Think of it as being on a fact-finding mission. Use this time to exercise professionalism and do not waste time and energy being bitter or rebuking the feedback. Assess what *is really* happening and use this as the opportunity to show that you are in control. What you do with the "feedback" is up to you.

What Leaders Can Do

Leaders carry the primary responsibility to make substantive changes so that women and high-performing men are considered for positions and promotions to a much higher degree than they have been in the past. Here are a few tips to set you up for success.

First, ensure that there is a systematic process for discussing and deciding on promotions. High-performing organizations promote the best talent, not just those who receive the most advocacies from their bosses or have been there the longest. Eliminate the loudest-voice bias to truly identify and promote the best talent and performers.

In addition, ask for potential promotion lists at least six months in advance so you have time to gain exposure to the individuals on the list. Most women, especially women new to the workforce, spend their time producing results while men cast a wide net of relationships, so engaging women and getting to know them before the conversation occurs is critical to finding your most talented employees. Also seek out high-performing men who fit the new, high-performing leader attributes and expectations at your company.

Deliberately create mentorships for high performers and women in the organization, especially recent hires. High-performing organizations encourage their leaders to invest in the next generation of leaders. Most mentors also state that mentoring younger leaders keeps them current, and they end up learning just as much from the mentee as the mentee does from them. Stay fresh while helping a woman thrive.

Things to avoid? Do not, do not, do not promote anyone who has distinctly imposter qualities like aggression, posturing, or a reputation for politicizing situations. Take a stand and do not allow these employees to continue to permeate your organization, even if removing them is unpopular or their boss could retaliate against you. Your job is to create a high-performing workplace for both women and men. Imposters are toxic and should never become part of the leadership of any organization, and if they are part of it today, they should be mitigated or removed (we'll talk about how a little later in the book).

If you have a deserving member of your team who did not get promoted, be candid yet supportive of them. One of your primary responsibilities as a leader is to develop your team. Women and high performers especially appreciate candor when given with the best of intentions. Follow up your candor with practical solutions and ask the members of your team to develop a plan so you can work on it together. In your next manager meeting, let the group know that you held the conversation (be an example to your peers!) and that you will keep them posted on any progress. Also let the team member know you did this, so they are encouraged to continue to progress.

As a leader, you have the power to make the shift within your organization, moving away from a place of not promoting women or high performers to an environment of equality and encouragement where the best talent leads the way forward (rather than an all-out war on talent where only the aggressive are left standing). It will take courage and leadership on your part, but it is required if you want to retain the most talented women and high performers for right-balanced, high-performing teams.

What Organizations Can Do

Maintaining fair and balanced systems of early promotions is critical to your overall success if you are an organization committed to creating a shift in the workplace to high performance. In fact, promoting talent and maintaining an organization's credibility are strongly correlated with organizations that experienced growth. Companies with high credibility are 2.7 times more likely to have grown over the past two years, and companies with top talent saw a similar edge, as they were 2.7 times more likely to have grown over the same period of time, according to Gallup.[3]

**Elements of the Five Conditions Framework
Strongly Related to Business Growth**

Companies with high **Point of View** scores are	Companies with high **Credibility** scores are	Companies with high **Talent** scores are
2.5x	2.7x	2.7x
more likely to have had consistent growth in the past two years.	more likely to have had consistent growth in the past two years.	more likely to have had consistent growth in the past two years.

GALLUP, 2019

Here are eight proven tips for ensuring that your organization is administering promotions fairly to the right high-performing women and men:

1. It all starts when the job is posted. Requiring a healthy balance of men and women applicants during the selection process is critical, particularly in male-dominated fields. The goal should be a nearly 50/50 split between male and female candidates.

2. Hiring classes, if possible, should have a nearly 50/50 male-to-female ratio.

3. Promotion requirements should be communicated during the hiring process, orientation, and one-on-ones. These requirements should include characteristics of a high-performing employee in your organization (i.e., a combination of both male and female characteristics, which we will discuss later).

4. All high performers should be aligned with managers who are skilled at identifying talent, not just for the next role, but for higher-level leadership roles. First bosses are especially critical

---

[3]Crabtree, Steve. "What Information Do Business Leaders Need to Bolster Growth? Gallup, February 10, 2020, https://news.gallup.com/opinion/gallup/285650/information-business-leaders-need-bolster-growth.aspx.

to a woman's trajectory in the workplace since they are more likely to focus on producing results rather than networking.

5. When discussing promotions, the person should be evaluated based upon the criteria communicated to them and discussed during their one-on-ones. Seeking multiple evaluations is a helpful way to ensure as much objectivity as possible. Only solicit feedback based on what was *expected* of the candidate during a specific time period and only from those who had substantive *exposure* to the individual's performance. Weed out any secondhand or general comments, such as "dropping the seed" of bad news about an employee (a tactic we'll discuss in detail later in the book).

6. Create career situations for women and high performers that provide exposure to different managers so they have a similar scale of feedback to the others during promotion discussions. Remember, imposters cast a wide net, so more leaders will know of them during discussions. Raise your awareness of hard-working and effective women and high performers by creating situations in which they are exposed to, and work alongside, other leaders. Cross-functional projects are a great way to view and to leverage talent in a new situation.

7. Before promotions are decided, cast a critical eye to the balance of men and women on the list. If you do not have a nearly 50/50 balance, women will have a more difficult time staying in the game. The key is to make sure that women are equally considered and discussed.

8. If a woman is not promoted, ensure that she receives specific feedback as to why and provide her the chance to improve or gain the exposure needed to be successfully promoted at the next opportunity, particularly if she has potential or a promising future with your organization. The same goes for any high-performing employee.

It will take more effort on the part of HR and leaders to administer the criteria across the board so that various subjective biases, such as the old way of promoting on potential, does not creep into decision-making.

For managers, it is also imperative to eliminate gravitas, internal overnetworking, bro codes, and other imposter traits from your selection process. These are unhealthy cultural norms that eliminate some of your best talent from the promotion pool, particularly women and high performers. Instead, include a balance of results orientation, leadership qualities, collaboration, and employee development into the equation and then use them to make the promotion decisions. You can find the high-performing leadership criteria in Chapter 13.

Early promotions are key to the advancement of women and high performers in the workplace, and losing out on them will continue to hold companies back. Organizations that want to take advantage of all the gifts these talented employees have to offer need to make sure their promotion mechanisms are fair and to take these systems of inequality into account.

Among the greatest threats in the workplace for high-performing employees, especially for women, bullies present some of the worst problems for all parties involved. Hungry for power and less concerned about productivity, bullies are both low-performing in their own work and detrimental for high-performing teams. The bad news is that bullies are embedded throughout corporate America. The good news is that a healthy, high-performing culture can take steps to remove or mitigate bullies and old norms, provided leaders are courageous and determined to make this shift.

7 | Removing Bullying from the Workplace

"I would rather be a little nobody than an evil somebody."
— *Abraham Lincoln*

For those who can break through barriers and ascend in an organization and in their careers, the toxic situations they encounter become much more pronounced, last longer, involve more people, and are more difficult to navigate. The higher you get, the higher the stakes. These situations are a result of low-performing cultures with toxic dynamics that allow their most aggressive, competitive, and incompetent people to push up-and-coming talent off their trajectory.

Fortunately for organizations, the people who are bullying are *not* your top performers and should not be treated as such, regardless of their political ties to leaders in your organization or their reputation. In fact, they are imposter leaders and should be thought of as such. An imposter typically has to use means other than their performance to get what they want because they are incapable of the actual requirements needed for the job. It's that simple. And when it comes to bullies, their chosen method to get what they want is intimidation and belittling.

These individuals bully their way into key positions, eliminating the true talent from the equation. Ironically, the true top performers do not need to use these tactics because their performance, leadership, and results speak for themselves.

Unfortunately, in today's corporate America, the bully often wins, typically because they are at a higher level in the company while toxic, low-performing cultures support their antics. Corporations usually don't figure out who the serial bullies are until it's too late, and by then the bullies have left a trail of carnage in their path.

Once organizations become educated on a bully's tactics, the bully immediately loses any power they might have over someone. The bully's goal, no matter their methods, is always to control the situation, and if they lose control of that, they will try to control how others see their enemy.

The opposite of a bully is a top performer. Top performers do everything the right way – they are strategic, drive results, lead with discipline, garner the support of their team, have high ethics and morals, design high-performing teams, collaborate with their peers, create win/win solutions, and develop and promote the next generation of high performers. This is the group that exponentially outperforms an average employee by increasing their results and the results of those around them.

Because they spend time doing everything right, remarkably, they become a target for workplace bullies – that's right, they become the *target* for workplace bullies!

Why? Because they are doing everything right and have everything the bully wants. The bully knows that the person they're bullying plays a fair game, but the bully has also figured out unfair tactics that will help them win a powerful position at their organization. The woman or high performer being bullied has respect, results, high-performing teams – and power – and the bully wants it. The bully has also predetermined that the one being bullied won't push back.

It is that simple.

It is the *organization's responsibility* to remove bullying from the workplace in order for their top performers and talented employees to ascend to higher, more impactful roles.

Here are some of the most notable tactics bullies use to eliminate competition and build their power in the workplace.

Discrediting

If someone becomes focused on discrediting another individual, it's a clear sign they have a problem and are using your organization for their own personal gain. More often than not, this individual has discredited others before, and it has worked for them. They've acquired departments, projects, or promotions by operating this way, so they continue using the same strategy.

For women and high performers on an upward trajectory, discrediting will cause angst and sleepless nights. It is a tactic used by bullies to reduce a colleague's value in order to increase theirs. It's a zero-sum game. Someone must lose in order for them to win. Those who typically seek a win/win scenario must keep in mind that the game being played is different – there is no win/win in this particular situation.

In business, character and performance matter. Women and high performers should protect their reputations first and foremost. That does not mean they should get overly aggressive or become someone they are not, or, worse yet, act like the bully. Mark Twain is quoted as saying, "Never argue with stupid people, they will drag you down to their level and then beat you with experience." The same can be said about bullies.

When dealing with a bully who is trying to discredit them, women and high performers should always stay in their highest and best character and handle the situation like the true professionals they are.

So, what does discrediting look like? Here's one story:

Cate was an up-and-comer in her company, receiving fast-track promotions and industry accolades. She was on the executive track and revered as a great leader, even at a young age, offering innovative solutions and gaining a fantastic reputation with clients. As Cate continued to make broader and increased positive impacts in the organization, she started to get noticed more and more. Executives began to talk about her.

Enter Doug.

Doug was an executive viewed as smart and driven, but was also known for taking credit for other people's work or getting others to question the performance of a peer in order to take over that person's department. Doing this, he acquired more power and responsibility, even though he was known as being a shady character.

Cate soon became an easy target for Doug when they became peers. At first, Doug was nice to Cate and showed signs of being supportive. He befriended Cate and quickly began sharing challenges within his department, asking Cate for her perspective. Little did Cate know, Doug was questioning Cate's performance with their boss behind her back.

Doug told their boss that Cate really wasn't strategic, the plan for her department wasn't working, and she wasn't cultivating and developing her top performers. Doug suggested he was the right one to step in and oversee some change. Doug began to "mentor" one of Cate's top performers and then started holding one-on-ones with people on her team.

Then Doug's big break came.

One of Cate's close family members passed away, and she was called away from the office for two weeks. It was all the time Doug needed to finally convince their boss that Cate was not quite the top performer that everyone claimed.

The boss began to look at Cate differently and started questioning everything Cate did. The boss began to hold one-on-ones with her direct reports, questioning Cate's leadership. Concerned for their own futures, her team regurgitated the narrative they were fed by Doug and the boss; that Cate might not be up for the job. Cate was on a downward spiral, even though her performance hadn't changed at all. She simply had someone who was successfully attempting to discredit her and questioning whether she truly was the star everyone thought she was.

If you are a strong performer, this *will* happen to you at some point in your career.

You become a threat to others who cannot measure up to you. They become jealous, envious, or simply want what you have. They will lie, cheat, and steal to get you out of the way.

When women are thrown into these situations, many tend to immediately think it was their fault. They try to rationalize and ruminate over what they said or did to make this person not "like" them. Unlike male high performers, who can typically detect what is happening, women struggle to hit the issue head-on.

Let me be crystal clear: it's not about liking or not liking or what anyone did or didn't do. Too often, women think it is much more complex than it is, trying to figure out how they messed up. Most high-performing men typically get this part right and can read the tea leaves. It's actually quite simple: it is the bully's issue. The bully found an opportunity and the woman or high performer became the target.

The Lying Peer

Another situation women and high performers encounter is a peer or executive lying in order to make themselves look good and the woman or high performer look bad. Because they are attempting to manipulate the boss or, worse, the leadership team, they will find something that the boss feels strongly about (such as whether others question his decisions or whether they like him) and lie about it. If the boss is not adept at recognizing these kinds of strategies, they may find themselves swayed by the introduction of misinformation.

Betsy's story is a good example of how this can happen.

Each year, planning for performance reviews began on October 1. At that time, not only were merits and bonus amounts decided, but promotions and organizational realignments were finalized. For nine months, Betsy had outperformed on all of her goals and had led her team through a difficult but positive transformation. Her team was high-performing and very engaged.

Unfortunately, her boss had a reputation as someone who had made it to the highest levels of the organization not by performing, but simply by knowing how to eliminate her competition. The good news was that the leadership, peers, and employees respected Betsy. She had delivered on everything that she and her boss had agreed to earlier in the year.

But her boss found her to be a threat.

So, she strategically began planting seeds of doubt right before promotion time, making up untruths about what Betsy had said to her and then sharing the untruths with key influencers on the leadership team. Although these untruths were inconsistent with Betsy's professionalism and personality, the team members didn't question her boss because of her position and reputation for being an executive favorite. The boss began to treat Betsy differently, questioning her in public, a clear sign she was no longer supportive of her.

In this situation, the other executives did not conduct their due diligence. The boss – their peer – was manipulating them because she had an agenda, and even though she had a reputation as someone who was willing to ruin an executive who was making a positive impact on the organization, no one was willing to step in and ask difficult questions. No one held her accountable.

In the world of business, this is allowed to happen every day.

It minimizes organizational performance and stunts the growth of the women and real high performers who experience this inequity.

Dropping the Seed

Highly political individuals use a cloak of secrecy to also discredit their "competition" and bully them in private. *Dropping the seed* is a tactic used to create doubt about another person.

A bully typically administers this by pulling their leader or someone close to the individual aside in a meeting or calling them privately. A few obvious approaches signal that someone is dropping the seed.

A bully might start by saying, "I really care about this person on your team, but I have to tell you, she is not doing well. In the spirit of helping her improve her performance, I wanted to share some insight on an experience I had with her." Typically, they'll follow this up with either an outright lie or discrediting half-truths.

Another approach might involve them asking questions like, "What is your take on Mary's performance? I'm hearing some things but wanted to check in with you. We have a great relationship and I want to help you any way I can." What they're actually doing is fishing for any bit of potentially negative information that they can exploit.

And guess what? Dropping a seed can be a technique that works. Why?

First, it's done in private. Quite honestly, if the person sharing the feedback was so interested in helping Mary, they would have provided the feedback in person, either directly with her or with both Mary and their boss. Or, as their leader, the other person would have let Mary know they want to share feedback directly with the team member.

Another reason this tactic works is because, most often, the feedback is never shared with Mary. Thus, the seed is planted and the targeted person is guilty in the mind of the leader. The leader becomes biased and begins keeping their eye out for risks or missteps. If they are also political or operating in primarily low-performing companies, this will signal to them that others do not think this person is a top performer, and they may not want to advocate for them, as it could make them look bad.

As this person's leader, they should consider themselves played.

Discrediting, lying, and dropping seeds about others are all typical tactics used by imposter leaders and the wrong up-and-coming employees and leaders to discredit competent, high-potential, or high-performing colleagues. If you are on the receiving end of these tactics, it's a clear sign you are a threat to the bully. Unfortunately, most women and high performers internalize what has happened to them, thinking it was their fault for their bad behavior or for not seeing it coming.

For women and high performers: This is not your fault.

It is theirs.

They are doing this to purposefully take you out of the game.

Do not let them win.

The timing of using these tactics is also a strategic move on the part of the bully. Because leaders are privy to leadership rotations, performance review discussions, and other crucial events in the business cycle, they time these drops to discredit you just before these discussions occur. Some may do it because they want to promote their own favorite person or because you have a department they want and the only way to get it is to put you down.

This should be your key takeaway: if this happens, there is a clear reason that the bully is using this tactic and it has nothing to do with your lack of performance and everything to do with them getting what they want. Either way, allowing an imposter to ascend and have a say in who gets promoted in a high-performing organization will cause whatever promotion system you are using to fail. This is why companies fail to promote the right people 82% of the time.

What Women and High Performers Can Do

If you are on the receiving end of any of these tactics, first and foremost understand why the other person is doing this: you simply have something they want and they can get away with it. They are willing to use unscrupulous tactics to minimize you so they can steal the limelight. It's an imposter tactic, so anyone using it isn't a high-performing leader.

Here are some keys to keep in mind when dealing with one of these situations:

1. Know that it happens and expect it to happen to you. Plan for it, especially if you are an up-and-coming businesswoman or high performer or have been assigned to a top project or position.

2. If a colleague is taking this approach, it is 100% a tool they have used in the past and have gotten away with. If this happens to you, speak to your leader about the situation. Keep it fact-based and brief. Let them know you have been made aware of a concerning situation that you believe was used to discredit you and that what was said is untrue. Do not let them talk you into being passive or not addressing the issue. The person needs to be exposed – sometimes you need to confront a bully in order to stop them from bullying again.

3. If someone shares with you that the bully was speaking poorly of you, an appropriate comeback could be, "Yes, I heard, but she does that to everyone, from the CEO to the mailroom, so I don't really give it too much credibility." This helps you retain your power in the moment and mitigates the bully's impact.

4. If the issue is pervasive, seek your boss's or HR's help in dealing with the person. But don't expect their overwhelming support, especially in a low-performing organization. They will view the situation as a risk to the organization and may want to move you to another role, making you feel as if the whole situation is your fault. They are avoiding the issue and mitigating their legal risk. You may want to begin weighing your employment options.

5. Journal every day and keep the journal at home. Documenting everything that is happening – who said what, at what time, in what room – will prove its weight in gold if something more sinister begins to occur and you're required to recite events. The journal will prove to be your best friend. It provides documentation, identifies patterns, and may also provide you with some wise self-coaching. It will help you keep the story straight and factual.

What Leaders Can Do

Most leaders are not immune to these tactics; in fact, most often it's the leader who is being used by the bully to carry out their plans. Don't become a player in their game by being manipulated by a bully.

In today's workplace, 360 feedback has become the norm. Asking others for their feedback on an employee's performance is normal in most performance management systems. Feedback, particularly from bullies, should be avoided at all costs.

If a leader is suspect of the feedback on one of their employees, the best way to determine its reliability is to ask the person you suspect of using an imposter tactic if the three of you can meet together to discuss. Ask them to share the feedback directly while you listen in to help the person create a plan moving forward. If they cancel the meetings, are no-shows, or are simply deprioritizing the information they had at first wanted to share, you should be suspect of their motives. Any leader should be able to provide candid, *helpful* feedback based on high performance expectations at any time.

What Organizations Can Do

The best approach for corporations is to implement the "three strikes, you're out" policy.

Leaders in your organizations should be the best and brightest. If someone is bullying to get what they want, if they're lying or discrediting or dropping seeds of discontent, they should be viewed as an imposter. The true top performers will never need to use a bully tactic to get what they want.

To create a "three strikes, you're out" policy, the board, leadership team, and employees need to be trained to Assess, Conclude, Tell (ACT)^{SM}. Every leader should be a mandatory reporter to HR and your HR teams should prioritize resolution. We'll touch on the specifics of this program later in the book.

All incidents should be reported directly to the CEO, and subsequently the board. No exceptions allowed.

The only way bullying can be eliminated from the workplace is if the organization acts by putting a name on it, prioritizing its resolution, and rectifying it.

To provide a healthy environment for top performers and women to thrive, companies must immediately remove any imposter leaders and their actions from their organizations. Educating and exposing their tactics will mitigate the bad behavior and put workplace bullies on notice that their old ways of posturing, bullying, and steering the organization no longer works.

Human resources, as part of and an extension of the C-suite and other organizational leaders, is critical in making this happen. They simply must introduce processes of mandatory reporting that include using ACT and the "three strikes, you're out" method, demonstrating to everyone that HR is driving the path to a new, high-performing culture.

Although addressing bullies and removing them from companies is vital for an organization's health and success, the challenges we face in winning the war for talent don't end there. In fact, the war on talent has a far more sinister element that we have yet to confront: narcissism. While this particular bully is among the most challenging to deal with, they cannot be overlooked as we move high-performing companies to the front of their industries.

8 | Removing Bullies in the Workplace: The Narcissist

Nobody can be kinder than the narcissist while you react to life on his terms.

– Elizabeth Bowen

Encountering a narcissist might be the most challenging bullying situation anyone will ever encounter in the business world. That comment is not made lightly, and it's not meant to give credit to narcissists, but rather to be honest about the wide-ranging, negative impact they can have on a person's emotional and physical health. Occasionally the timeframe of the encounter is limited, but most often narcissists will subtly wreak havoc on you personally and professionally over a long period of time.

To appropriately navigate a narcissist and come out the other side stronger requires first fully knowing a narcissist's motives, learning how to identify them, realizing what their insecurities are, and understanding that they will use whatever tactics are necessary to get their way.

Narcissists 101

True narcissists have narcissistic personality disorder.

Narcissistic personality disorder — one of several types of personality disorders — is a mental condition in which people have an inflated sense of their own importance, a deep need for excessive attention and admiration, troubled relationships, and a lack of empathy for others. But behind this mask of extreme confidence lies a fragile self-esteem that's vulnerable to the slightest criticism.[1]

Narcissists are typically very bright and are the owners of their universe. In their mind, everyone is beneath them, including their boss, but they know how to make them feel important, manipulating them into a sense of being respected and admired. Narcissists typically have very large and expansive vocabularies and use them to impress others, especially executives.

Narcissists consume other people's energy to make that other person feel weak. The definition in the dictionary is as follows:

Narcissist: noun

1. A person who is overly self-involved, and often vain and selfish.
2. Psychoanalysis. A person who suffers from narcissism, deriving erotic gratification from admiration of his or her own physical or mental attributes.

As bosses, narcissists expect 100% loyalty. If at any time they determine someone is on the fence about them or is not fully

---

[1] "Narcissistic Personality Disorder," Mayo Clinic, https://www .mayoclinic.org/diseases-conditions/narcissistic-personality-disorder/ symptoms-causes/syc-20366662. Accessed May 28, 2020.

supportive of them, they immediately will move to discredit that person and use whatever behavior they feel necessary to let them know that they are no longer in their good graces. Yelling, secret discrediting tactics, slamming their fists on a desk, berating, avoiding accountability, boomerang blame, and minimizing are all part of their process to eliminate the perceived threat.

Here is a quiz to get a better handle on whether a boss is a narcissist:

The Narcissist Quiz	Y/N
1. In their first encounter with you, did they try to reel you in by telling you a sob story (i.e., a nasty ex, child abuse, bad friends)?	—
2. Regardless of the situation, do they make themselves look like the victim?	—
3. Do they create drama to draw attention to themselves?	—
4. Do you feel something toward this individual you've never felt about anyone before, such as overwhelming empathy, loyalty, or disgust?	—
5. Do they try to isolate you from your other friends?	—
6. Do they gaslight? Bully you, then make you feel special behind closed doors, then berate you in public?	—
7. Do you feel like you're always second-guessing yourself or feel off-balanced around them?	—
8. Are they overly competitive and nothing in your life comes close to what they are dealing with or have dealt with?	—
9. Do they root for the underdog in public as a way to garner attention for themselves?	—
10. Do they make up lies about grandiose encounters?	—
11. Does all the attention need to be solely on them and if it's not, do they act out and turn the attention back to them?	—
12. How do they treat someone who pushes back on them? Does that person become a target of their toxicity?	—

If someone exhibits at least half of these behaviors, they may be a narcissist.

Continuing to work or deal with a narcissist is a zero-sum game. Their co-workers have to lose in order for them to win, and they will stop at nothing to make that happen. They will lie, cheat, take credit for other people's work, hide when they are called out, and quickly become the victim, soliciting the sympathies of executives and peers while continuing to make others the villains. Unfortunately, they are adept at becoming part of the executives' inner circles, and from there they can manipulate a variety of situations.

Most executives and companies do not understand that a narcissist wreaks havoc on organizations, minimizing the value of those around them and eliminating talent pipelines. Companies also do not understand that narcissists do not care about the company or the executives; rather, the company becomes a means to an end for them, a feeder for their own self-gratification and a battlefield where their "wins" can be played out in a public forum.

Why do companies keep narcissists? Because narcissists are also visionaries. They can see things others cannot, and because they can schmooze and make the executives feel good about themselves, they have a tendency to have a long lifespan at a company.

It often feels like a nuclear blast could not eliminate narcissists from the spaces they lodge themselves in within organizations.

What Women and High Performers Can Do

If you encounter a narcissist, here are some options to consider:

Run. Like you have never run before. Seriously. Especially if you are an up-and-coming talent who is admired by others, has a great reputation, or are in the middle of building a reputation. Narcissists seek out anyone who has anything they want, and if you are adored, that makes you a priority for attack. Because they have an insatiable desire to consume you, draw you into their drama, and make you out to be a bad guy, there is no winning with a narcissist, particularly if they are at a higher level. Severing any ties with them is the first step.

Be a diamond. Sometimes you must work with a narcissist – as a peer, boss, or executive. It may be that you're at a point in time at which you cannot leave your job. Then what do you do? The first step is to design an exit strategy, immediately. The longer you have to deal with this person, the worse your life will become, especially if you are a peer or employee. As you are creating the exit strategy, think of yourself as a diamond (bright, multifaceted, and impenetrable) when dealing with this person. You can do this by minimizing any interaction, physically moving away from them in the office, and minimizing your calls with them. If you must interact, try to do it in groups or via email so they cannot manipulate the situation. Whatever you do, do not react to their tactics in an inflammatory way. That only provides fuel to the fire they are creating.

Manage your reputation. Document everything in your journal – every conversation, everything you hear, and every person who talks to you about this person. The narcissist does not deal in facts, so having documentation is critical; facts cannot be manipulated. Once you have these facts, alert your boss to this individual's desire to discredit you and ask for their cover. If your boss will not help, go to others in your circle and let them know this is happening and ask for their help. Typically, this has happened to other people and they can provide guidance. The more you can out the narcissist, the better. Also consider going to HR and asking for their guidance. Keep in mind that if this person is at a high level, and your HR department is weak, they could make the situation worse, so understand your risks before approaching them.

Reach out. If you are in a vulnerable position (e.g., are new to an organization), contact mentors outside of your workplace who know you and let them in on the situation. Also consider contacting an attorney in your state so you know your rights.

What Leaders Can Do

If you are a leader of a narcissist, you will feel a great deal of loyalty from them. They will make you feel like a smart, one-of-a-kind leader and will support you among your peers and the C-suite. Defending and protecting you is their biggest charge in their professional career (or so they make you think).

Great bosses do not need to feel so safeguarded or protected. An executive who needs that level of protection is actually exhibiting tremendous weakness. If you identify someone on your team who is making you feel this way, it would be best to find out why. What bosses of narcissists need to know is that they *do not* have the capacity to care about others. They are only using these tactics to gain your support, adoration, and endorsement to continue to rise in the organization in order to gain more power.

As a great leader, your role is to create an inspiring culture where each and every person is motivated to succeed. If you have a narcissist on your team, it is virtually guaranteed that you are not achieving that mission. Your role is to identify your imposter leaders, remove them from leadership roles, and replace them with great leaders who will keep high performers in your talent pipeline.

If you don't, you become part of the problem.

What Organizations Can Do

Organizations cannot continue to be high-performing for a long period of time if they employ narcissists, unless the narcissist is corralled into a role that does not allow their toxicity to permeate the masses (such as Steve Jobs, the second time around at Apple). The best way to eliminate a narcissist from your company is not to hire one in the first place. Identifying a narcissist, particularly those under consideration for executive or leadership levels, during the interview process through personality assessments by a trained professional is a must if you are building a high-performing culture.

If there are narcissists within an organization, everyone needs to assume that this person is wreaking havoc wherever and whenever they are involved; therefore, they need to be closely managed. Don't expect employees to speak up, at least the ones who like your company or their jobs, because they will live and operate in constant fear of retaliation. The narcissist has proven enough times that they will eliminate anyone who stands in their path and will use that fear to keep others quiet.

As mentioned earlier, organizations can minimize the damage by keeping the narcissist in roles that are visionary and largely individual-contributor roles. All feedback or insight the narcissist provides on other employees or peers should be viewed as highly suspect and discounted immediately, as they are only able to approach these situations from their own selfish point of view. That is why these individuals are so toxic to the real high-performing talent pipelines. Anyone, at any level, who they perceive as challenging them – their status, position, or role, or anyone they view as competition – must be eliminated. And these individuals will be your best performers.

Any complaint to HR by an employee should be taken very seriously and, once again, fall into the "three strikes, you're out" policy, along with ACT^{SM} mandatory reporting. Expect the narcissist to deny everything and to place the blame on the person receiving their abuse and bullying. But don't fall for this. The word "accountability" does not exist in narcissists' extensive vocabulary and you need a very strong HR person and boss to hold them accountable and keep them corralled. Over time, they will find the limitations exhausting and go elsewhere, but not after they try to take you down as well.

Narcissists are one of the great landmines in American business culture. Knowing what to look for, and what to do when you're forced to work with one, will go a long way toward helping organizations create high-performing teams and helping women thrive in their careers.

Another variation of bullying in the workplace that appears far more subtle than the narcissist is the politician, who craftily schemes to manipulate others. Politicians are motivated by power and influence, and they will use subtle tricks to achieve their ends. If a company isn't prepared to spot the tactics of a politician within their ranks, many of their most talented team members are likely to suffer setbacks, to say nothing of the company's external competitiveness.

9

Removing Bullies in the Workplace: The Politician

"There is no limit to the amount of good you can do if you don't care who gets the credit."

– *Ronald Reagan*

Mark grew up in a family of politicians. He was the mayor of his local town and, through connections, quickly became a young senator. He was adept in the ways of politicians, creating alliances to promote his agenda and discrediting anything that would compete with his vision or his power.

Mark eventually left politics to parlay his skills into the corporate legal world. After serving in this capacity for 10 years, he wanted a promotion. Mark needed to expand his department and responsibilities to get to the next level, so he set his sights on a new junior partner, Natasha, who had been given tremendous responsibility. She was poised, professional, a great leader, straightforward, and had a great deal of integrity and character. She quickly won over her peers and collaborated effectively with them. She was constantly giving credit where credit was due – setting up her peers, bosses, department, and even the CEO for success. No one ever heard her say "I" or "me." It was always about the client, the person on her team, or her direct report. She empowered others and, for that, she was viewed as a tremendous asset to those who worked with her.

Unfortunately, she also had responsibilities that Mark wanted, and he had the new CEO's ear multiple times per day. He knew the CEO would not take them away from her, so his strategy was to discredit this high-performing junior partner and make her seem less than she actually was, and he had the power to do it.

Mark began to work more closely with Natasha, telling her they could partner on a few projects that would benefit both departments. He had little to no background or expertise on the projects, but he could play more of a sponsorship role and help her get them pushed through with the partners. He would instruct Natasha to leverage whatever resources she needed, even those on his team, to develop a plan. She put a dream team together, including members of his team, and she and Mark developed a strategic yet highly executable plan to achieve their common goal.

During Mark's one-on-ones with the new CEO, he mentioned that he was working closely with Natasha but that she was struggling to move the project forward. People on his team were complaining about her leadership, and she could not provide them with appropriate direction. His team was doing all of the work. He told the CEO that he would keep a close eye on it but wanted to let him know about it just in case he had to take over the project. Seed number one was dropped in Mark's political plan to oust her.

The CEO had no idea that it was all a lie. Mark had contributed nothing to the project up to that point, and none of his team members were complaining. In fact, the opposite was true: no one, not even Natasha, could get ahold of him, and he offered no direction or input but was quick to present the basis for the project at the executive meeting.

Once the team put the plan together, they held one more meeting to finalize the approach. Mark came to this meeting and Natasha gave credit individually to each person around the room, saying that it was an innovative solution and that the group should be very proud of their accomplishments. The team would present the findings to the CEO shortly.

Mark left the meeting and later that night added one item to page two, put his name on the title page, and sent it to the CEO, stating that the original project did not meet his expectations and therefore he had had to redo most of the work. He also stated that at the final team meeting, Natasha took all of the credit for the work and did not given any to his team (all of the good parts were his team's ideas, he said). He said that he was very disappointed in this Natasha and was questioning whether her department should be in charge of this new undertaking. Mark suggested they discuss the project at his one-on-one.

A few days later Natasha set up a meeting with the team, the CEO, and Mark. The CEO responded that Mark had already presented a variation of the proposal and he was ready to move forward. Mark's department would take over the execution of the work.

Not only did Natasha do all of the work, including cross-departmental leadership, and not only did she do everything right, she had lost the opportunity to execute the plan to someone whose only goal was to eventually take over her responsibility.

This project should have been executed from her department but she would always support anything that was in the best interest of the firm. She wanted to better understand how the decision was made, though, so she included the topic as a one-on-one agenda item with the CEO.

In the interim, she attempted to talk to Mark directly to find out what had transpired. He was continually unavailable or would accept meetings and then not show. Mark proceeded to announce the changes and because he did not have anyone on his team to actually execute the project, he approached one of her team members (unbeknownst to the female executive) to recruit them to his department and execute the project. Natasha started piecing all of this together and she figured out Mark's shenanigans. She felt better informed for her one-on-one with the new CEO.

In the one-on-one with the CEO, she solicited feedback on the proposal. He stated that he approved Mark's proposal. He understood that Mark was disappointed in where the project had landed and had had to redo everything. Natasha asked to see the proposal and quickly determined that it was virtually the same one presented to Mark. The CEO thought it was best for her to set up a time to meet with Mark, as he also was very critical of how she had handled the project, saying that she did not give credit where it was due and took the project in the wrong direction.

The CEO was not a well-versed politician, and he was not adept at dealing with members of his team who were completely self-serving. It was as if he couldn't comprehend that someone would operate that way. To know that both leaders were partnering and then accept a proposal from only one of them, regardless of the reason and without the other's consent, was unacceptable leadership behavior.

His antennae should have gone up immediately, and he should have questioned everything he was being told. As the ultimate leader in the organization, he set the tone for how Mark and every other partner or junior partner would behave. If he allowed Mark to operate in this manner, this would be how Mark would operate externally, with clients and with regulators. Mark was a risk to the organization and his behavior needed to be addressed.

Most executives and CEOs would chalk this up to Mark being Mark, or say that this is how it is done. Mark wanted the promotion and was aggressive in pursuing it. But just because someone wants the power does not mean they deserve it or are capable of doing it (Mark did not really want the work). This is a perfect example of why executives who are not fully capable of running the business are sometimes promoted to the highest level of incompetence. It was simply because Mark knew how to manipulate his boss and the low-performance infrastructure.

What Women and High Performers Can Do

Politicians in the workplace are slippery. Their lies can be infuriating and their game annoyingly juvenile.

If you have been targeted, first and foremost, call the person what they are: a politician. Putting labels on bad behavior is a must if an organization hopes to transition into being a high-performing organization. Labeling the behavior also sends a signal to those around you that this person cannot be trusted and exposes their game, forcing them to refocus on what matters – healthy relationships and industry-leading results.

Second, reiterate your core beliefs to the highest person in charge who has heard this nonsense from the politician. Let them know that this person is communicating untruths and that your behavior has been nothing but above board at all times. Some leaders on the receiving end of a politician's game are selected because the politician does not think they will be called to the carpet. Regardless, offer to have a meeting with the three of you to set the story straight; just don't expect a politician to tell the truth. Be prepared with the facts and your expectations, expectations employed by high-performing teams.

What Leaders Can Do

First and foremost, do not label these problems as personality conflicts or refuse to engage. If someone on your team is using these tactics, they are playing you and are using other employees for their own personal gain. It is in your best interest to hit this issue head-on in order to stop the politician's bullying. This behavior has no place in a high-performing organization.

In this scenario, a great boss, first and foremost, would have established ground rules for their executive teams, which would include expectations from each leader and what role they play on the team. Together, not individually, you will achieve your goals. They will be judged on the merits of impact and leadership, not on political acumen, deceit, or gravitas. If he or she catches anyone operating in this manner, they will be put on the "three strikes, you're out" program. It is amazing how the culture of an executive team and a company can change when the leaders set the tone.

Another option is to have both leaders meet in your office to determine what happened and why. You can reiterate your expectations and use this situation as a learning opportunity. This will signal to the politician that you are on to their game and that you have no place for that on your high-performing team.

If you do suspect a politician on your team, know that their loyalty may lie with you at that time, but the reason they are so good at what they do is that they can play a new side at any time to serve their own purpose. It is difficult to truly believe what they tell you because everything is distorted and in the best interest of getting what *they* want. Affinity relationships are key to them, so they typically associate with whoever has the highest power. If that is not you at any point (most leaders are in the doghouse at some point in their career), don't expect them to stay, because you are simply a means to an end for them.

What Organizations Can Do

Politicians, like narcissists, have behaviors that are counterproductive in the workplace. They are one of the biggest time wasters in corporate America and they have difficulty driving tangible results, thus the smoke-and-mirrors tactic.

Politicians, like narcissists, only stay at an organization where they can manipulate, particularly up the leadership chain, so identifying, corralling, or removing the individual is imperative to achieving high-performing teams.

For a trained HR professional, politicians are easy to spot and even easier to manage. Once they are questioned, they are easy to back into the "corner of truth" because their story will not make sense, and the lies will compound other lies. Even they won't be able to keep their story straight.

Because these individuals identify with many derailing characteristics, they need to report to a strong high-performing leader who can keep them focused and on task. Once they are focused, most politicians find the leader stifling and will choose to leave, but they will try to paint an unflattering picture of the leader or their performance before they leave. All information at this point should be suspect at best.

Politicians can unleash chaos in an organization if they are allowed to continue operating in their deceit, especially in an organization not prepared to deal with them. But they are also easily suppressed in a well-organized, high-performing company because the structure and operation of such a company will reveal their lies and manipulations quickly.

HR should make sure that the right processes are in place, and they should also be prepared to ask difficult questions to identify a politician. Once exposed, they will either fall in line or find your company too stifling, and they'll leave on their own.

While some bullies are crafty and difficult to spot, other bullies and their tactics are much easier to catch if you know what to look for in the heat of the moment. The tactic of baiting an employee is common among bullies who try to get a colleague to say something critical of colleagues, the company, or executive leadership. Once high performers and leaders learn to spot this practice, they will be prepared to respond appropriately and to take action.

10

Removing Bullies in the Workplace: Baiters

"A fox is a wolf who sends flowers."

— *Ruth Brown*

Baiting is another tactic used by imposters to throw competent performers off their game. Baiting is the act of attempting to coerce an opponent to say something or act in a way that is inconsistent with their historical performance or beliefs. Baiters will, through any means necessary, try to get you to react in a way that will get you into trouble or shine a bad light on you in the eyes of leadership.

Baiting in Your Organization

Early in her career, Mollie was promoted to senior manager, a role typically reserved for individuals who had been with the organization for at least 10–12 years. She was five years out of B-school but had accumulated an impressive resume of accomplishments and results. She was driven, authentic, bold, and an awesome leader of people. Employees from around the organization wanted to work for her and to be on her team. She was known as ultraprofessional, unflappable, and honest.

Because she was an executive with only a few years of experience, other more seasoned executives would typically bait her to try and set her on the wrong course or to get her to say something inconsistent with corporate values so they could begin to paint a much more sinister picture of her and take her off of the upward trajectory and fast path to the executive suite. In Mollie's current role, her department was responsible for the branding of the organization, so she typically worked with senior leaders to develop and execute communications – to clients, employees, and policymakers. Every communication went through her department.

Mollie had been in the role for about a year when the organization began to fall on hard times. The economy was sluggish at best and sales began to decline. The executive team had to make some tough decisions regarding raises and bonuses, as well as promotions. As the head of branding, Mollie was part of those discussions. The firm had historically taken a strong stance against layoffs, but because of the severe downturn in sales, they had to put them on the table.

Layoffs were put on the executive meeting agenda. A week earlier, Mollie had a meeting with one of the executives on another topic. They began to discuss how their departments could continue to work together during the downturn and possibly share resources if the company moved forward with layoffs. Although a serious conversation, it was professional and the executive appeared very open to a stronger partnership.

The executive then asked her whether they should move forward with the layoffs. Mollie's response was balanced, straightforward, and articulated the impact a layoff would have on their brand.

The executive then responded, "So you are saying that you do not agree with any layoffs and that it could run this company in the ground!"

Mollie replied, "No. What I am saying is there are pros and cons to any decision and a layoff will have downstream impact not only to our employees, but our core belief system and culture. And it could land in the press. As the steward of our brand, these are all consequences we need to discuss and debate to ensure we make an informed decision."

The executive continued, "So what you are saying is that you disagree with the executive team and think we are stupid for even thinking about a layoff. We aren't thinking about it the right way and you are going to tell them so. In fact, you look like you are ready to go tell him now. Does that make you angry, because you sure look angry? I think you need to settle down."

Mollie laughed and stated that she looked forward to the conversation with the larger group and cut the conversation off and changed the subject. The executive was clearly attempting to bait her into saying something negative about her peers. He was also attempting to make her angry and act inconsistent with her historical professional demeanor.

Clearly the executive was putting words in Mollie's mouth. Because the incident happened behind closed doors, the executive could misrepresent, misstate, and lie about the conversation, which he promptly did with the team that afternoon. In fact, for dramatic effect, he visited each person on the executive team to tell them about the false conversation and recommended that Mollie not attend any of the meetings because she was too emotional and dramatic to have a professional conversation. Although inconsistent with every engagement the executive team had had with Mollie, they passively agreed. Mollie was disinvited to the meeting and the company moved forward with the layoffs. The story landed on the front page of their local city newspaper and all industry publications, which she promptly had to address as the head of public relations as well.

Baiting situations are typically evidence of a greater plan to discredit you, so consider it a warning shot across the bow when it occurs. Because a baiter is attempting to discredit you, the best approach is to remain calm and professional as you articulate your position.

When Mollie eventually found out what had happened, she approached the CEO and explained that she had prepared a comprehensive branding downstream impact plan, complete with pros and cons, of a layoff decision. If heard, it could have changed, or, at a minimum, more strongly informed the decision. The CEO stated that the executive had shared with him that Mollie was incapable of having a professional conversation about the topic because she had gotten heated and emotional when speaking to the executive the week before.

Mollie laughed and stated that the executive had attempted to bait her during the conversation. This wasn't her first rodeo, and it was clear what he was attempting to do. She refocused the conversation to touch on the root cause of the issue, which had little to do with her. She asked if there was any reason why this executive would not want the executive team to hear about the impact to the brand.

The CEO stated that this executive thought he could do a better job at branding (although he had no formal training or experience!) and that Mollie wasn't needed. Mollie stated that the behavior the executive described was inconsistent with any of her previous approaches to a decision that could impact the brand and asked that the next time the three of them have a conversation to ensure that all sides of the story were represented before a decision was made. The CEO agreed to this approach.

Although Mollie fell victim to baiting that time, hopefully it would not happen again.

As you can see from the previous example, baiting typically occurs during the course of a light-hearted or everyday conversation. Once a baiter has you at ease, they begin their maneuvers. At first, it might be a mild attempt to twist your words, and they may use phrases like, "So you are saying. . . " before pressing you in a way that will elevate your blood pressure and push your hot buttons. They may make completely untruthful observations during the conversation to get you to argue with them, such as in Mollie's case, where she was accused of saying things she never said and acting in ways she never acted. Once the other person attempts to portray the situation contrary to what is happening, you know baiting is in play.

It's nefarious, underhanded, and all too common in today's low-performing companies.

What Women and High Performers Can Do

The key is to quickly identify when baiting is occurring, take a deep breath, and regroup.

One quick tactic you can use is to ask them their opinion. If they answer honestly, then they might be looking for an honest conversation, but if they quickly dismiss your question and continue pressing you with inaccurate observations, they are baiting you.

When that occurs, look at your watch, do a time check, and state that you hate to cut this short but must leave. Then tell someone, ideally a mentor you can trust, about your encounter. Your next step is documentation.

Document the time, place, and conversation – everything you remember. This will serve you well if the conversation is used against you, like it was with Mollie.

The key to working with someone who is baiting you is not to be accessible to them in private. Baiters work one-on-one, so being in a group setting is your best defense.

If the nature of your working relationship forces you to have one-on-one time, use this three-step test to quickly determine if you are being baited:

1. Did the conversation start off cordially and with positive rapport?
2. Is the other person playing back your conversation inaccurately?
3. Did the tempo of conversation become quicker and more aggressive?

If the answer to these questions is yes, you're being baited.

To ward off a baiting attack, use this three-point approach:

1. Identify the tactic.	Once you know the game, you can identify the next step.
2. Remain calm.	The reason for the tactic is to get you to say or do something out of character. Don't take the bait.
3. Manage the outcome.	If this person lied about the conversation, use Mollie's approach as a guide to shed light on the situation.

What Leaders Can Do

Many women and some high performers have difficulty identifying tactics being used against them. As a leader and possibly a mentor, helping to put a name on the tactic is helpful. Once a woman and high performer can identify the tactic, they can resolve it with less emotion and frustration.

If you are a leader, here are a few tips to deal with a baiter:

1. If the person being baited is on your team, there needs to be a conversation between the three of you: you, the baiter, and

the baited. Facilitate the conversation to reach a conclusion on what transpired. At a minimum, this puts the baiter on notice.
2. Determine what the baiter had to gain by doing this to the other person. Was it a power play? As a leader, this will provide invaluable insight into how they operate and what their next steps might be. There is always a next step, because baiting is part of their larger plan.
3. Keep your eyes open.
4. As a leader, also be prepared for the baiter to begin discrediting you as well. If they cannot control you, they will control the situation, so be on guard.

What Companies Can Do

At their core, baiters are deceptive people and baiting should be considered a warning sign of larger issues with them. At a minimum, baiting, like other bully tactics, should be added to your "three strikes, you're out" program *and* your derailer list (which we discuss later in the book).

Baiters need to be refocused on their roles and performance. Like other bullying tactics, they are spending more time trying to manipulate than in performing for your organization and shareholders.

A strong HR department or leader should be able to easily identify this tactic and send a warning to this individual that this is unacceptable behavior, and that leaders in the organization are expected to act with the highest integrity and honesty. Depending upon the topic and how they were using the baiting situation, this could become a formal performance warning, either bringing about a change in behavior or ushering the baiter one step closer to termination.

While baiting behavior can drain valuable talent out of your pipeline, it's relatively easy to spot and to counter. The ongoing damage can be minimal if identified and handled properly.

However, this is not the case when it comes to illegal tactics and abuse in the workplace. The blast radius and long-term damage of abuse and illegal tactics are extremely concerning, while the day-to-day damage to a company's culture can accumulate over time. Every high-performing organization needs to effectively eliminate this behavior – and people – from the workplace sooner rather than later.

11 | Removing Illegal Tactics and Abuse in the Workplace

"The greater the power, the more dangerous the abuse."

— *Edmund Burke*

Over 75% of American employees have experienced a tumultuous situation at work and defined it as abuse. Abuse is just as pervasive as bullying but has a more profound, negative impact to the individual and the workplace. Certain forms of abuse have been deemed illegal and movements like #metoo have created awareness and advocacy to eliminate abuse from all workplaces.

Abuse in the workplace may show itself in a physical form, such as sexual abuse or physical harassment, but most often the most pervasive emerging trend is the mental abuse that is inflicted upon employees. Mental abuse can happen at any level in every industry, and the trauma of workplace abuse can affect the abused for years to come, to say nothing of diminishing the excellent performance of your top employees.

Why Abuse Happens in the Workplace

Let's be bold and clear about why abuse happens in the workplace and where the accountability lies: it happens because organizations do not hold abusers accountable.

Period.

This accountability is the responsibility of the board, executive leadership team, and human resources. Yes, the abuse in an organization might be limited to a single abuser. But for someone to carry out abuse, it is implied that abuse is tolerated, otherwise the abuser wouldn't still be there. Over 70% of women who report abuse in the workplace are retaliated against. Without the appropriate rules and boundaries in place, abuse will become an innate part of the way things are done, and more and more situations will arise the longer it goes on.

It's that simple.

Employee Agreements Perpetuate Ongoing Abuse

The advent of employee nondisclosure agreements has become a cloak of secrecy for workplaces because, although abuse happens to a majority of American workers, few complaints reach the public. Why? Because employers force American workers to sign these legal documents as a condition of employment, silencing the abused from warning others once an incident occurs. Should an individual sign those agreements, they are severely restricted in who they can disclose abusive situations to. You are unable to post anything on social media or third-party work sites. You are legally bound not to tell your friends.

As a result, the abuse continues.

The agreements you sign also put you at a disadvantage from the very beginning because they typically state that if there is an illegal issue reported to HR, mediation will be called in to find a resolution —mediation that is often appointed and overseen by the employer.

And so, the abuse continues.

Illegal Tactics Used in the Workplace

Consider Aaron's story, someone from middle management in a US-based company.

> When I first was fired from my job, I contacted an attorney who had been recommended by a friend who had a similar situation at the same company. The first question the attorney asked was whether anything illegal had happened. My knee-jerk response was to say no, not that I know of. For me, it was just a very unprofessional situation and I was fired from my job. Thankfully, I was in my right mind and asked him what is illegal in our state. He went on to articulate the usual suspects: age, sexuality, religion. But my situation wasn't any of those. He told me I didn't have a case and sent me on my way. After conducting my own research, and speaking to another attorney, I found out that what happened to me *was* illegal and I was able to negotiate a settlement with my former employer.

Most individuals work in a "right-to-work" state. These laws basically state that the employer, or employee, has the right to terminate your employment at any time. But what it doesn't state is that the *way in which* an employer terminates you, or the *process* used to terminate you, may be illegal.

Here are a few examples of illegal tactics used to terminate an employee:

Setting You Up for Failure

This is a tactic often used at the executive level, but it can be used for other team members as well. The goal is to create situations where you cannot succeed so that managers can blame you for the inability to produce results, and then let you go for "just cause," giving them the opportunity to pay you less severance. Managers executing this tactic typically use the element of surprise and baiting to set you on a downward spiral.

They may show up at your desk and state quickly that they would like you to head up a certain project and it must be completed in a very short period of time, much shorter than it would take Superman or Wonder Woman, then quickly walk away. They will become unavailable for questions or make it appear that your questions are completely out of line. For example, they may be pleasant to you in the morning, then surprise you with a call into their office that afternoon and verbally abuse you for asking stupid questions. They may do this several times in a short period of time, thus creating a story line to finally fire you for performance while making you think you are a failure.

Their goal here is to manufacture a situation in which the company does not have to pay you severance or unemployment, because it is for "just cause." However, the truth is, it is all a ploy to defraud you and the government (by not paying unemployment benefits).

The Poor Performance Review

Ricky was a 20-year veteran of a large corporation and had received the highest performance rating for her work and leadership for the past 16 years. By all accounts, she was a star performer – well-liked, respected, and a great leader. She also had a quality relationship with her boss. A little over 18 months earlier, the department was realigned to a different side of the business and her boss was placed under a new boss. Soon after that, her boss's demeanor began to change. She wasn't as open as she used to be and seemed on edge.

That year, Ricky was surprised to receive a middle-of-the-road appraisal rating at year-end. No warning, no discussion, and suddenly she went from being considered a top performer to average in less than six months. At the next mid-year discussion, she received the lowest rating. When Ricky asked her boss why, she gave an answer that placed the blame on her own boss.

Two months later, the boss pulled Ricky in and told her she was fired for performance.

Eliminating Your Position

Occasionally, the company will come to the conclusion that they want to eliminate your position, but in order to pay you little to no severance or unemployment, they make you *think* it is due to performance. They may use similar tactics for poor performance or setting you up to fail, or they could simply manufacture poor performance stories that aren't true.

This is a telltale sign your employer is using illegal practices or processes to fire you.

What Women and High Performers Can Do

In any of these situations, it can be difficult to think clearly. The behavior, requests, and allegations can be shocking to the system. Regaining a clear head and making sense of it all is critical. Here are some tips to help you:

- **Use ACT**: *Assess, Control, and Tell.* From the first odd encounter, assess the abuse in the first instance. Once you identify the tactic, it is much easier to do the next step.

- **Remain calm at all times**. Nonperformance is often used as a reason to let an employee go, but there is a legal process that must occur in order for the employer to prove that the firing truly was performance-based. Therefore, most often, the person who is abusing their power and creating an illegal situation cannot reinforce their allegations. When your manager pulls you into what appears to be a toxic situation, remain calm and ask the question, "What would you recommend I do in this situation to remedy the issue?"

  Their response will tell you everything you need to know.

  If they cannot or will not offer a solution, or if they tell you to do something that is completely illegal or not in alignment with your employee agreement, you know you are being set up.

- **Document everything in your personal journal**. Include dates, times, conversations, what was said, and how long the conversation lasted. Most employers will block you from taking any documentation from the workplace after you are fired, including voicemails and e-mails, so this documentation will prove its weight in gold should you ever engage an attorney.

- **If you are truly being fired for nonperformance, there is a process an employer must follow**. This includes using the performance management system found in the company's employee handbook with the goal of helping you perform at your current role. If there are deficiencies in your performance, they should offer you training and a reasonable time period to turn your performance around. Become very familiar with that process in your company and if it is not being used, you can suspect you are being set up.

- **Engage an attorney immediately**. They will be able to provide you with direction and insight into what is legal and what is not, your legal recourse, and who is within the purview of legal action. Depending upon the situation, bosses or other executives could also be sued personally, so it's not just the company at risk.

- **Start looking elsewhere**. If this is how your boss – and company – handles situations, you do not want to work for them anyway.

What Leaders Can Do

There is a right way and a wrong way to fire employees or to reduce your workforce. Never become that leader who is using illegal tactics, regardless of what your employer is asking you to do. You need to know the right way to reduce your workforce, as you personally could be sued as well, so never stoop to abusive tactics in order to fulfill your company's wishes.

As a leader, your role is to create and to uphold the best possible culture within the organization. If you are made aware of illegal tactics being used to reduce the workforce, consider it a warning to *you*, because if they do it to others, they could just as well do it to you. The best thing for you to do in order to protect yourself is to find other employment and not engage in these illegal activities.

For leaders in the most egregious situations, whistleblowing may be your only option. Contact an attorney if you have decided to use this approach. There are certain steps you need to take, and you'll need the advice of an attorney to consider all of the pros and cons.

Always remember that, as a leader, your reputation is built over the course of your career. One illegal act can take you off an otherwise positive trajectory.

What Organizations Can Do

If you allow abusers to use your company and your employees for their personal or professional gain, you are at risk. As more employees become aware of illegal tactics used in the workplace and are willing to take legal action, your company's future success will depend on your ability to create a high-performing and inclusive culture. Making the shift to a high-performance culture should become an imperative at your organization.

If you allow the abuse to continue, inevitably your organization will experience peril. Legal situations caused by abusers (and bullies) can lead to large monetary settlements, public scrutiny, reduced sales, and a tarnished brand. These situations are difficult to recover from and can be the demise not just of the abuser but of the company as well.

To create high-performing cultures and organizations that maximize the talent of every employee, particularly women, bullying and abuse need to be eradicated from the workplace. Bullies and abusers are simply using your organization for their personal self-gratification, so not only are employees losing, your company and shareholders are losing as well.

Using the ACT approach, you can educate all of your leaders and employees on how to identify, approach, and eradicate bullying and abuse from your workplace. With those barriers to high performance removed, you'll be prepared to redesign your workplace so that your top talent can thrive. By making this shift, you'll prepare your company to produce better results than you can imagine today.

PART III

Redesigning the Workplace

12 | How to Make the Shift

"To change ourselves effectively, we first had to change our perceptions."
— *Stephen R. Covey,* The 7 Habits of Highly
Effective People

    The workplace has changed and true high-performing leaders are prepared to take companies to new heights, leading their teams through a variety of different methods that develop their strengths, create impact over the long term, and create highly engaged, happy teams. The fundamentals of leadership have changed, and for companies to succeed in the future, it is imperative that they hire, identify, and then promote those leaders. If a company begins to change its criteria and to remove the barriers that block high performers, the next step is to figure out how to make sure the right people are promoted and identified in your pipeline so that your culture can continue to shift toward high performance.

You can use this five-step process, using the acronym of SHIFT to create a step by step guide in your organization. The five steps are:

S – Start with balance at the top
H – HR's new role in the high-performing company
I – Identify high performers and potentials
F – Focus on a five-year plan
T – Track and communicate your success

S – Start with Balance at the Top

What gets measured gets done, and to be successful, companies should have specific goals with well-defined time periods within which to achieve them. For example, some companies have a five-year goal to add women from the C-suite to a 50/50 gender breakdown in hiring classes. The board should lead the effort by setting realistic but challenging goals for the organization; the executive team will be held accountable for executing and achieving the desired results within a specified time period.

The best strategy to create a high-performing movement is to hire the right women in key positions from the very beginning, from the C-suite through other key leadership positions. Here's why: to create success, women need to lead the transformation *alongside* men. The men in the C-suite are not women. They do not think like women, they cannot be a substitute for women, and if you want women to succeed, women have to help bring about this new high-performing culture (remember, right-balanced, high-performance expectations are a blend of the best male and female traits, so both genders should help design and execute the shift).

The executive team should also immediately be assigned to mentor and sponsor other women and men who have been identified as high performers based on standards we will discuss in this chapter. This will reinforce the new expectations for the executive team and help educate and guide the mentees to also exhibit the new set of high-performing rules, creating a real-time shift within the organization. Making this basic, first move shows the organization and the outside world that you have commitment and focus.

Creating Integrated Expectations

The need to create this balance at the top of an organization and then filtering this shift down through the rest of the organization will only grow more urgent. Today, there are over 74.6 million women in the workforce and more women than men are graduating college. It's not enough to add new, promising talent to organizations. Rather, leaders need to *integrate* this talent into their new high-performing expectations. How? The first step is to acknowledge that men and women have different innate characteristics that, when combined at the highest levels through entry-level positions, create a high-performing organization.

There are basic and innate differences between men and women; they each have their own talents that can drive companies to industry leadership. Today, it is taboo to talk about these differences between men and women, but to create high-performing cultures, this fundamental topic needs to be discussed, illuminated, and embraced.

Here are the most pronounced differences and common trends and tendencies experienced in the workplace:

Boys and girls are encouraged and raised differently. It all begins with our American culture. Boys are encouraged to be competitive, to get out there and win, and to be rough while they do it, while girls are encouraged to be nice, play well with others, and get along, all while remaining smart and driven. These distinct differences play themselves out through adults in the workplace.

Women compete with themselves, while men compete with others. For most men, business is a competitive sport. Women, on the other hand, view work as a team effort and a way to make a difference and drive results. Whereas men are competitive with others, women have a tendency to compete with themselves.

Women listen more, while men use gravitas. Men take up more space in meetings and speak 75% more than women when in a group, according to scholars at Brigham Young University and Princeton.[1] Women are typically reserved, thoughtful, smaller in stature, and take up less physical space.

Women like strategy; men like facts. Women use process, think in multifaceted ways, and place a higher value on strategy and intuition (which may lack facts). Women also take into account downstream impact whereas men like to deal in facts.

Women are promoted on the basis of results, while men are often promoted based on potential.

Women use the word "we," while men use the word "I." Men tend to perpetuate the notion that something was their idea and that they directed every facet, eliminated obstacles, and achieved great results. The use of "I" means that only *they* deserve the credit for success and solely led the charge. Women tend to use the word "we," giving credit to the team as a whole. The translation of "we" is that everyone contributed evenly and that success only came because she had a great team working with her.

Men define career success by achieving a job title, while women define success by results. Men are risk takers and the more success achieved, the more testosterone their body produces.[2] Success is their fuel for more success. Women define success by being great leaders, organizing teams to drive impact and results. They have a high degree of empathy and develop top talent. They are nurturers.

---

[1] Mendelberg, Tali, Christopher F. Karpowitz, J Baxter Oliphant, "Gender Inequality in Deliberation: Unpacking the black box of interaction," Princeton University, Feb 7, 2012, https://scholar.princeton.edu/sites/default/files/talim/files/Gender%20Inequality%20in%20Deliberation%20-%20PDF.pdf.

[2] Van Edwards, Vanessa, "Gender Differences: 6 Fascinating Differences Between Men and Women," *The Science of People*, https://www.scienceofpeople.com/gender-differences/, Accessed June 8, 2020.

Here's a chart highlighting some of the differences between male and female trends. I understand that not all of these fit every woman or every man, but their impact and presence has created our current corporate culture.

This is probably a good place to address our nonbinary and transsexual coworkers. Maybe you were born a gender you no longer identify as. For you, these lists might seem too cut and dried, too binary, but my main point in all of this is that we need to change the expectations to acknowledge the majority of workers today.

Male Trends	Female Trends
Encouraged to be competitive, to play to win.	Encouraged to be nice, play well with others, get along, are less aggressive.
View the workplace as a competitive sport.	Work is a team effort, a way to make a difference and drive results. Are nurturers, not competitors.
Want the best for their organization.	Want to drive results for their organization.
Use gravitas, take up more room, and speak 75% more than women in meetings.	Are typically reserved and thoughtful, take up less room and speak less than men.
Use facts to make decisions.	Use process, are multifaceted, and talk out loud; take time for decisions.
Promoted based on potential.	Promoted based on results.
When discussing credit, they use "I."	When discussing credit, they use "we."
Define success by their job title.	Define success by results, team success.

Male Trends	Female Trends
Are risk takers. Success is their fuel.	Have a high degree of empathy and develop top talent.
If overdriven for success, they can become overly competitive. If threatened, can become a bully.	Are typically targeted by overly aggressive or competitive peers and leaders, both men and women.
Aggressive behavior is natural and rewarded.	Are suppressed by aggressive behavior and if they use it toward others, are viewed unfavorably.

The Answer?

High-performing companies will start with balance at the top and incorporate it throughout their organizations by integrating the best of male and female characteristics to develop high-performing leaders. This is where the true opportunity lies for organizations to succeed in the future.

There are men and women in the workplace who are great leaders today, are supportive of their teams, and want the best leader to succeed, but even they are not fully versed in or understand the differences in this new, next-generation high-performing culture. Even if they did, they cannot make the shift to a more balanced workforce alone or from the bottom up.

Making the shift to high performance starting at the top and working down throughout the organization will set you up for success since leaders will model the change that needs to happen. As of today, most companies have men playing by rules they've always played by, and women, who have rarely been exposed or treated in an aggressive manner in other arenas of life, are entering the workforce and struggling. And there are women already in the workplace trying to figure it all out as they attempt to climb the proverbial corporate ladder. Each group has little education or insight into the strengths of the other group, let alone how to respectfully work together and create high-performing teams.

Corporate cultures are not truly valuing or fully leveraging the strengths women bring to the table. **Women today are being hired because of their innate talents, but judged on an antiquated hiring or performance system, which, in effect, mitigates the value and diversity they bring to the organization.**

For companies to succeed, an integration of the best innate traits of women and men must define tomorrow's expectations of high performance. It will take the adoption of new expectations and a new type of HR leader who can lead an organization through the transition.

H – HR's New Role in the High-Performing Company

Major initiatives in any organization start with clearly defined goals and roles. The goals identify where they are going and the role(s) identify who is accountable. Both are an incredibly important part of any company's successful shift. We'll discuss the goals in a minute, but for now, it is a good time to address who should be ultimately accountable for the shift: the board, the CEO, and, ultimately, the head of human resources.

High-performance organizations believe that their people are their greatest asset, but without someone ultimately accountable for their overall performance, organizations develop their own set of cultural norms. I have seen this decentralized leadership play out over and over again over the past 30 years, causing silos of individual expectations and subcultures within organizations. Exceptional talent needs exceptional leadership in order to thrive. Similar to other roles in the C-suite, the head of HR should have ultimate authority and accountability to exercise leadership over the human capital. Today, most organizations leave conflict management and resolution up to each manager and if HR gets involved, they lack the power to create accountability, particularly of their leaders. Putting HR in the driver's seat will ensure that your newly established norms are executed consistently across the organization from the C-suite to entry-level positions.

To execute across organizations, there should be a newly established HR department and its infrastructure should include (but not be limited to):

- **A highly respected leader or industry-leading professional to lead your HR department.** This individual should be strategic and have a proven track record of leading and developing high-performing organizations and human capital transformations. They should have a seat on the C-suite and would ultimately be responsible for all aspects of human capital leadership and management, including all goals related to high performance (gender balance, high-performing leaders, and women). They would be responsible for reporting all ACT complaints directly to the CEO and board of directors and would make the ultimate decision on any changes, including firing, elimination of positions, and rotations of leaders and high performers, with board approval. Decisions would be guided by the new high-performance infrastructure expectations and not solely by the legal risks to the organization. When selecting this position, don't discount the great leaders who are currently within your leadership ranks. They've been part of the culture and know how to effectively lead. If they are already a great leader, the transformation would have instant credibility and support from the teams – and the other high-performing leaders.
- **A highly competent coaching team to train and instruct leaders and teams on the new expectations.** This team would also be responsible to be a go-to for all ACT complaints or coaching and have the authority to make resolution

recommendations to the head of HR up to – and including – terminations of low-performing leaders.

- **Hiring, at all levels, will become increasingly important in a high-performance organization.** Selecting individuals who have aligned character traits, beliefs, and leadership behavior consistent with the new high-performance expectations will become a top priority. The recruiting team will have the final say in the hiring of individuals, similar to a GM on a professional sports team.

- **HR would implement the data and metrics that would be used to determine the progress within the organization,** including a leadership dashboard that would be used for development and promotions of leaders, team engagement, and any personality assessments at the organizational and individual levels. These metrics would feed into the corporate dashboard.

- **HR would work in conjunction with the CMO to ensure that the external and internal branding and communication are in sync.** This relationship will be one of the most critical to your organization, because, in some industries, brand drives over 60% of buying decisions. The alignment of your people to the external brand messaging is critical in a high-performance organization.

- **A comprehensive performance management system, which includes benefits, pay, merits, and bonuses.** Part of this responsibility will ensure that there is gender-equal pay and that the performance management system is executed consistently and fairly across the organization.

For companies that currently have relegated their HR department to overseeing benefits and the administration of payroll, they will need to reinvest in a strategic head of HR role. Companies can hire from the outside, or this person could be a high-performing leader from within the organization. In terms of return on investment, this will be one of the highest-impact positions within your organization for the right person who can successfully execute the shift.

Once you have the right people at the top and in HR who are empowered to move your organization toward high performance, you'll be prepared to identify who the high potentials and high performers are within your organization. Getting the right leaders in place and promoted within your organization will be crucial in making the shift.

13

Identifying High Performers and High Potentials

"Knowledge is the process of piling up facts; wisdom lies in their simplification."

— *Dr. Martin Luther King, Jr.*

The third step to creating a high-performing culture includes identifying and promoting your highest performers and highest potentials. This role should be shared by every high-performing leader and employee in the organization and should be established by an industry-leading set of high-performance standards. High-performing employees are two to five times more fiscally valuable to an organization than other employees and contribute 91% more in achieving business goals.[1]

---

[1] Newman, Greg, "How Can We Better Identify HiPos Using Network Data?" *Trust Sphere*, April 5, 2017, https://www.trustsphere.com/identify-hipos-using-network-data/.

To be competitive, you can't just identify these employees – you must honor your new high-performing culture by retaining and promoting them.

Twenty-five percent of high potentials are planning to leave their company within the next year, while the other 75% are 10% more likely to leave than other employees.[2] Keep in mind that most leave because of bad or toxic bosses, so if you replace those bosses with high-performing ones, you should begin to see immediate improvement in retaining your top talent across the organization. Then these high potentials must be effectively honed to meaningfully contribute to the organization while also reaching personal goals.

Remember, high potentials are different than overachievers. Overachievers can achieve great results but often leave "dead bodies" along their path, are hyperfocused on winning at any cost, and are politically savvy. They are the bullies and abusers, so make sure your organization can tell the difference between them and the talented high potentials.

The best qualities of high potentials or high performers may not be apparent at first since they tend to produce results quietly, at least compared to their more toxic peers. A high performer will be driven by the following personal qualities:

- Strong personal character.
- An appetite for learning, growth, and generosity.
- Internally driven.
- Positive but realistic.

You may not notice these qualities right away, but they will soon lead to results that you can't ignore:

- Their teams will be engaged and inspired.
- They flawlessly execute their projects.

---

[2]Ibid.

- They deliver consistently superior results over time.
- They are respected as inspiring leaders, both internally and externally.

High performers are also typically targeted by non-high performers to weaken their performance in the organization. It will be imperative that once your remove-and-replace strategy is set, there is a systematic and consistent approach to your decisions. We'll cover that soon. For now, the following are a few strategies that will help you decide on an approach to shift toward identifying and retaining high-performing leaders and potentials and minimizing the impact of low-performing leaders that will be best suited for your organization.

Selecting the Right High-Performing Leaders

The individuals selected for your high-performance leadership roles should have *core characteristics* needed to build and lead highly engaged teams that produce outstanding achievement in their current role.

High performers and high potentials exhibit certain personality and character traits exhibited by both men and women, including grit, ethics, integrity, drive, and teamwork. They achieve great results through a combination of establishing a vision, tying each member's contributions to the team goals, and developing their team members.

In essence, they are a prism through which every team member's key talent shines. This makes them great leaders.

These leaders also do not engage in office politics, bullying, abusing, or any of the derailing characteristics we have identified. When the competition heats up during the transformation, they are the ones who are worried most about their teams and clients, not themselves. Even during these times of transition, they will find positive and meaningful ways to keep their team members focused and progressing toward accomplishing the organization's goals.

As companies create this new high-performing workplace, all of the existing leaders within your organization will need to be reevaluated based upon this new set of standards, because they will be the group critical to evolving your workplace culture. The CEO sets the tone for your company culture and can create upwards of 50% of brand value in the marketplace. To make a change in your organization, the CEO must exhibit the qualities of a high-performance culture. The new, high-performing leaders will be asked to eradicate pervasive aggressions, bullying, or workplace abuse, so it is also key to ensure that they are well trained in the new expectations so they are empowered to make the change happen.

As you are redesigning your leadership team, remember: one bad apple can spoil the whole bunch and can poison your efforts for positive change, so retaining any negativity, including the bullies and abusers in the workplace, will be a detriment to success. Also, by removing toxic leaders from their roles, it shows commitment to the new culture. Your team members know exactly who these people are because they've wreaked havoc on them and the workplace for years. This cannot be reinforced enough: identifying and removing them is critical to your success.

High-performing leaders exhibit the following traits:

- They have a winning combination of impeccable character, leadership, and results over time.
- They are driven by *we*, not *me*.
- They are in constant pursuit of the right answer for the organization. They do not need to be right.
- They are constantly learning and growing and striving to become better through each and every experience.
- They must have people skills, be altruistic, and act with humility.

- They must remain coachable and make nonideological, nonemotional, and nonimpulsive decisions.
- They are often quite "boring" individuals, not hounded by scandals, and are very predictable.
- Their teams have clear expectations at all times.
- They exhibit integrity, authenticity, and ethics.
- They are not self-centered, but are team- and company-centered.
- They are masterful at identifying and leveraging each team member's strengths and talents.
- They enjoy giving credit where credit is due.
- They expose conflict, with the goal of creating win/win solutions to resolve it whenever possible.
- They find joy in their people succeeding.
- They are risk takers and are willing to take a stand for their beliefs.
- If there is ever drama around them, they are usually the target and not the one who started it.

Remove Low-Performing, Imposter Traits

During a transformational shift, non-high performers will find the change to be a hit on their livelihood and position. They will begin to act out in a variety of ways, from using attachment to higher-level leaders by deepening their personal relationships to using overly aggressive and underhanded tactics to discredit their peers who they perceive to be a threat. HR and the CEO need to be able to identify these derailing behaviors and confront the reality that these individuals are not the high-performing leaders needed for the organization's transformation and will need to make the tough decision to cut them from the team. A strong HR executive and team will be critical during these times and throughout the transformation process to make sure that low-performance behaviors aren't allowed to undermine the new high-performing culture.

Low-performance behaviors are defined as personality traits, actions, and character flaws that will derail individuals and the organization from high performance. Exhibiting these traits is a clear sign to leadership that the individual is not a high-performing leader and should be watched consistently to minimize their impact on their teams and those around them. Unfortunately, most derailers are personality traits that are difficult to change, so if you identify them in your current leaders, the mission becomes one of off-boarding rather than rehabilitation. Based on the ground we've covered in the previous chapters, here is a simple evaluation tool you can use to determine if a leader is a great fit for your high-performing company or if they are insecure and tend to derail others. You can use a simple grading system where you check each quality, add up the checks at the end, and then consider whether your leader is taking your team toward low performance.

Check If Observed	Low-Performance Behavior Checklist (Derailing Behaviors)
__	Being untrustworthy or unethical, even in the most minor circumstances.
__	Building an inordinate number of relationships with key decision makers versus with their peers.
__	Uses the word "I" when discussing accomplishments or progress.
__	Does not take risks.
__	Competes with peers rather than focusing on the company's competition in the marketplace.
__	Uses bullying or abusive tactics with others; gets worse as they are watched or outed.
__	Does not take responsibility for actions, mistakes, or lack of results.
__	Wants to win at all costs.
__	Exhibits aggressive behavior (yelling, overtly challenging, diminishing others), including bullying or abuse.

Check If Observed	Low-Performance Behavior Checklist (Derailing Behaviors)
—	Makes decisions one-dimensionally or in their personal or professional self-interest.
—	Does not share information in order to diminish a peer's ability to succeed.
—	Manages through intimidation, punishment, and directives.
—	Is not inclusive and cancels one-on-one sessions and does not engage daily with team members and leaders.
—	Is not approachable.
—	Seeks to be right in situations rather than doing the right thing.
—	Asks questions in group meetings to show dominance and power instead of providing information or truly seeking to understand or solve a problem.
—	Disengages in meetings (e.g., puts their head down, checks their phone, whispers to others, rolls eyes, acts bored, uses intimidation such as overstaring or loud sighs).
—	Is narcissistic; creates drama so that they can become the solution, expects 100% loyalty, and when they view someone as a threat, they use unscrupulous tactics to diminish them or to get them to leave the organization.
—	Uses illegal tactics to remove team members or leaders from the organization.

Every organization has its own unique culture, so use this list of low-performance characteristics as a starting point for employees and leaders to consult and modify together. That way, your list is unique to your culture. When it is built together, more people are accountable to govern and ensure that these behaviors are identified and curbed. This low-performance characteristics list should

be used as part of the evaluation criteria in your employee handbook when determining who will be hired, who is selected as your
high performers, and for performance reviews each quarter.

If a current leader exhibits at least two of these characteristics, they should immediately be put on watch. As the pressure gets
turned up, they will more than likely begin to exhibit more of these
derailing traits and should be immediately removed from any type of
leadership position. Chances are, they have exhibited these traits in
the past but have learned how to navigate the past political climate
and relationships to remain a leader.

How Promotions Work Today

It was October, the time for year-end promotion discussions, where
managers from throughout the organization got together to battle
for the few promotions available. Dustin had been through a few of
these discussions and always had someone on his team he managed
to get promoted. He felt confident that the two names he had on the
list, Patrick and Randy, would achieve the same fate. He knew how
the game worked and had "shopped" the names to those around
the table ahead of time. He had also made sure to give them credit
for projects under their guidance. He thought they showed promise
for what the company needed in leadership – they were aggressive,
driven, took risks, were very competitive, and did a good job getting results. Yes, they sometimes burned bridges, but that is what it
took sometimes to get the job done. He had heard rumblings from
other managers that Patrick and Randy weren't good peers, but he
chalked that up to the other managers being jealous. He thought
that if you are going to survive and get ahead in this organization,
you have to be tough – it's not about whether people like you; it's
about getting to the top seat and having power, and you got that
by having people around you who have your back, especially when
things go wrong. He was in that inner circle himself and wanted

to make sure the people being added were just like him. He felt Patrick and Randy were perfect additions to the inner circle and would easily fit in.

During the meeting, the managers took their turns talking about the people they wanted to promote. Little time or conversation was given to whether the job had expanded responsibilities or whether it was a role that would drive higher ROI, create less risk for the organization, or create higher client satisfaction. Instead, they focused on the people. Presentations of the nominee focused on criteria such as gravitas, impact, power, competitiveness, and "cultural fit" for leadership. When it came to Dustin's turn, he stated that both Patrick and Randy deserved promotions because of their hard-nosed, result-driven approach. Both had proven over the past year that they wanted the leadership role – exhibiting competitiveness, being driven, taking risks, and pushing their people to get the job done when needed. He was especially impressed with their ability to "manage out" certain people who were not a good fit for the organization, which meant they were too soft and couldn't take the pressure on their teams. No one questioned Dustin or his criteria for judging their performance, or whether these characteristics were the right ones for the leadership standards established by HR. Those weren't used anyway. In the end, both Patrick and Randy were promoted.

What happened next after this promotion? In most companies today, it's likely that high-performing employees who were less aggressive or well-connected but performed with all the attributes of a high performer either grew discouraged or began to seek a position in a different company. It's also quite likely that Patrick and Randy continued to alienate their colleagues and to drive their teams hard toward achieving ambitious goals. While they may have delivered results, the costs may have begun to mount. In addition, Dustin may have found himself managing the conflicts they created or worrying about replacing the talented team members who quit due to Patrick or Randy. Perhaps Dustin viewed these challenges as the price to pay in the business world. The more subjective the bias, the more this promotion system plays itself out. The result? The company finds itself in a war for talent, but in reality it is truly fighting a war on talent. There's also a good chance that a competing company is going to figure out how to retain talent, promote better leaders, and work toward reaching goals more efficiently. Executives focused on the bottom line and on maintaining a competitive edge will begin asking if managers like Dustin should be trusted, let alone retained.

HR Evaluations Provide a Consistent Measurement

In a high-performance organization, HR plays a much greater role in the identification, selection, and rotations/development opportunities of all talent, but more importantly their high-performing talent. This eliminates the majority of subjective bias with existing leaders as well, creating a renewed focus on the people, clients, and organization.

HR will have a variety of tools in their toolbox and can determine which survey or tests are best to identify the innate drivers. Enneagrams, Myers-Briggs personality tests, or interviews are a great way to determine personality strengths. Gallup's Strengthfinders 2.0 is another great tool for smaller organizations to use that identifies current strengths. (Keep in mind that it will identify the strengths they are using at the time and can change over time and with different roles. For example, an individual contributor may have more strengths centered on detail or influence, whereas a leader may have strengths aligned to results and empathy.) High performers can draw upon a vast repository of strengths, deploying them in a variety of roles – the definition of talent in the high-performance workplace.

Using both qualitative and quantitative methods for selecting your high performers will help you identify your diamonds in the rough, create a more robust talent pipeline, and provide each aspiring high performer a road map to success.

Great HR leaders can leverage a personal dashboard and key measures as a starting point for their organization. The HR leader will also be central to the execution and ongoing administration of the program.

The Case for Data-Driven High-Performing Companies

The evidence, both from independent scientific studies and from studies exploring the drivers of effective corporations and business resolve, shows that companies that are more meritocratic, less nepotistic, less political, and more data-driven in their talent identification processes end up with leaders with a higher IQ, a higher EQ, and skills that lead them to outperform their competitors. They also have higher revenues, higher profits, and higher market cap. Their staffs are more engaged. They have higher net promoter scores. They have higher productivity and innovation indices.

There is no secret; the ROI is there.

Meritocracies are the ultimate goal of the new, high-performance workplace, creating environments that exude energy and creativity, connectivity and collaboration, all of which lead to outstanding shareholder value. If your organization started on the meritocracy path and took a left turn into the low-performance cul-de-sac, you can get it back on track. In order to create a meritocracy, boards, executives, and HR must lead the transformation of their organizations.

Creating a high-performance culture isn't difficult. It's achieved by implementing a set of behaviors and norms that lead an organization to superior results by way of setting clear, long-term, and sustainable business norms and goals. These help to define employees' expectations, both in their roles and how they interact with each other, which in turn creates a trusting environment and encourages employees to continuously develop and grow.

But the benefits of a high-performing culture go beyond simple ROI. These environments embody an energy that makes employees want to come to work each day. The leaders are inspiring and empower those around them to be their best, setting ground rules and goals for the entire team that lead to their collective success. In a high-performing culture, colleagues are ethical, fun, and collaborative. They know the sum is greater than the parts, and each person is willing to give more than they take.

As an executive, it's easy to think to yourself that this already describes your company. But remember, very few companies are actually high-performing organizations. Most organizations were born out of internal competition, which has led to tactics that reduce the productivity of the workforce, cause turnover, and will eventually yield untold numbers of lawsuits as younger generations encounter the workplace. This anti-bullying generation will not tolerate today's corporate cultures and, instead, demand high-performing leaders and peers who work toward a common goal together. If you especially want to win the war for talent by hiring *and* retaining women, real high performers, top leaders, and future generations, a high-performance culture will be required.

This change will not only be positive for your entire organization, but possibly yield better bottom-line results as well. If you sit on a board, are in the C-suite, or are an up-and-coming executive, your competitors are finding every way they can to compete against your organization and win. Shifting to high performance will provide you the momentum needed to stay in the game and to beat out your competition over the long term.

Companies are under immense pressure to change or become irrelevant. Thankfully, this change is easier to bring about than you might think.

One of the most critical decisions you will make during your shift to high performance is the selection of your new high-performing leaders and potentials within your talent pipeline. Based on employee feedback, today's organizations select the wrong leaders over 80% of the time. To make an impact, high-performing companies should have a goal to select the right high-performing leaders at least 90% of the time. To achieve this goal, companies will need to remove subjectivity and bias, replacing them with both qualitative and quantitative measures. This will increase objectivity, while removing bias and putting your organization on a path to high performance. Here's why:

Today's leadership selection process is mired in antiquated methods, causing companies to pick future leaders of their organization based upon subjective insights, including the guidance of imposter leaders who aspire to find underlings just like them – or worse. Dustin's story was a perfect example of the subjective process used today to select leaders, leading to why employees believe the wrong leaders are selected over 80% of the time! For most companies on a quest to create a leadership pipeline or that aspire to create high-performing teams, this leadership selection process is the one thing that keeps them from achieving success, let alone progress.

Qualitative and Quantitative Methods for Leadership Selection

The marketplace has advanced, particularly in the area of technology and data and analytics over the past 30 years. Machine learning, algorithms, and predictive analytics are making the sales cycle shorter, targeting the right prospective customer at the right time during the buying cycle. Phones have tracking devices and can anticipate your next move, serving up the time it will take you to get to work each day. Some will even provide you the fastest path to take.

Technology has also been proven to accurately identify new high-performing leaders and the talent pipeline. Using what we know about past and predictive behavior, what can be learned versus what is innate, and how advanced methods of identifying your true high-performing leaders and talent will help you find the diamonds in the rough. Using data and analytics will take your organization on a completely new path toward industry leadership, while removing over 80% of your subjectivity bias used in today's promotion decisions.

The key to any successful transformation is a balanced qualitative and quantitative selection system using an individual dashboard that would be created, updated, and managed as part of the new centralized HR infrastructure. This will remove your antiquated approach to identifying and promoting imposters while replacing them with new characteristics of high performers.

The Individual Dashboard

Each leader and high potential in your organization should be represented on a personal leadership dashboard that includes both the qualitative and quantitative measures of the aggregated performance up to this point in time.

If you think of a typical company dashboard, on the left side are the drivers and on the right side are the outcomes. Individual dashboards using both qualitative analyses as the drivers and quantitative methods as the results side of the equation are a good tool to increase the objectivity of your selection of leaders. Here's why: qualitative methods predict success for a given population but in order for you to put this process to good use in your organization, you need to align these individuals to positions or projects that leverage their strengths, help them grow and develop, and provide them with challenges to overcome in order to maintain and evolve their confidence to ultimately succeed at higher levels. That will ultimately help drive the right side of the dashboard, or results. Selecting the right individuals for the right projects or leadership will be critical to developing and progressing your talented high performers. To build the dashboard, you need to use objective measures to evaluate both qualitative and quantitative aspects of an individual's performance.

Qualitative Measures

Qualitative analysis measures the quality of the subject or data; quantitative analysis measures the quantity. Quantitative analysis looks to facts, which could be represented by numbers. One theory that applies to human performance is that using the combination of both qualitative and quantitative data is stronger because the limitations of one type of data are balanced by the strengths of another. The two different methods are integrated to make the two distinct methods stronger.

There are a variety of studies that have used predictive analytics to identify the qualitative drivers or key criteria of high performers in the workplace. Studies have shown that qualitative characteristics are innate to the individual and are highly correlated to predicting successful leaders. Innate talent also drives real results. High-performing leaders with these innate talents increase profitability, productivity, and employee engagement, with women driving higher results than their male counterparts. They include the following.

Innate Talents of High Performers
- Character and personality
- Leadership skills
- Intellect

Character and personality. This is first and foremost the one thing that most companies pass over, but it is the *most important* when it comes to high-performance leadership! Character and personality are ingrained traits that are an individual's moral compass combined with an ambition to succeed – the right way. These traits are innate and difficult to change. High performers exhibit the highest ethics, integrity, and morals. Their guidepost is always to do the right thing, *regardless of the impact on them personally or professionally*. They have an appetite to learn and grow. They are open to new experiences and have the wherewithal and courage to remain persistent in the most challenging circumstances. They are measured, calm, and positive but also exhibit passion and humility. They are trustworthy. They exhibit grit, perseverance, strategy, positivity, risk taking, and balanced confidence. A high-performing leader's personality is one of the greatest predictors of their success. Trained HR professionals can proactively identify these traits in current and potential leaders. Some coaches and organizations use the Enneagram quiz or the Myers-Briggs Type Indicator to find leaders' personality traits. These assessments are fairly inexpensive and provide a great deal of information to help leaders better understand an individual's personality traits, when they perform at their best, and when they don't. These will be key in helping you select your leaders of the future.

Leadership skills. There has been an ongoing debate about whether true leaders have innate leadership skills or whether they can be learned. Today's research would tell you that innate leadership characteristics are the best predictor of success and that identifying the right leaders and cultivating their already innate skills provides companies a fast pass to leadership success. These leaders, first and foremost, want to lead people. Company results are an outcome of the power of the combined talents, energy, intellect, ingenuity, innovation, and thought leadership of their team. Leaders know that the sum is greater than a team's individual parts and they are seamlessly able to leverage each person's unique talents in combination with others' in moving toward a common goal.

These leaders inspire individuals and groups with a profound mission and established expectations on how they will accomplish it together. They proactively identify possible impediments to their success, and establish how they will respectively resolve conflict. They are respectful – to everyone, not just those at higher levels. They proactively give praise and recognition in public and coach and develop in private. They inspire each person on their team to do their best every day, because they expect their best every day. When there is a gap in an individual or team's performance, they seek the root cause, not assigning blame or pointing fingers. This new leader is who everyone wants to work for and be developed by, and is identified as one of your top leaders in your organization.

In addition to Gallup's Engagement Survey, high-performing organizations should also ask individuals for a list of the top 20 leaders they would work for in your organization (or outside for that matter!). Why? Aligning individuals to those leaders who inspire them to do more, be more, and produce more both identify the leaders you want to consider as high performers or potentials but also helps you identify the alignment of people to create high-performing teams. The one drawback to this approach? Old-world leaders of the past will have an opinion that this is a popularity contest and that this isn't truly reflective of their leaders' skills. In today's high-performing teams, the people know who the great leaders are and who they aren't. At the most fundamental level, isn't a large part of leadership about leading people? Asking for the top-20 list is just one more data point the C-suite and HR can use to identify high potentials.

To bring all of this together, use the following acronym as a starting point to identify your high performers or potentials: GREATNESS.

G – Growth, of both your business and people.

R – Recognition, of their peers, people, and organization.

E – Execution with empathy. High-performing leaders can balance both.

A – Accountability and accessibility. They are ultimately accountable but always accessible to their people.

T – Team builder and developer. They are constantly looking for ways to bring people together for a common good.

N – Noble. This person has high moral principles and ideals, combined with humility and candor.

E – Ethics and wisdom. They use ethics as their base for every decision.

S – Strategic and visionary. High performers and potentials see around corners and can anticipate next steps. They are also creative and envision a future that is different than today's reality.

S – Self-aware. They are adept at self-awareness, understanding, processing, and learning how they impact others.

Intellect. There are several studies on this topic and most land here: Leaders simply need to be smart enough: too smart and you are found unrelatable to the people you are leading; not smart enough, you could be viewed as incompetent. Typical IQ tests that ask an individual to solve for a three-variable calculus equation or the Pythagorean theorem are funny at best and tell you more about the subject's interest in math than their ability to be a high-performing leader. Tests that evaluate an individual's ability to solve problems, proactively identify opportunities, and strategically identify how to move your organization forward given the complex world we live in is a better predictor of success than a standard IQ quiz. Instead, IQ tests should be replaced by evaluating an individual's grades. Studies show that grades are a better predictor of success because they require a combination of the ability to learn, resilience, perseverance over time, and accomplishment. Trained psychologists and experienced HR professionals can easily identify the right tool to use for their organizations. Before any organization gets too focused on intellect, refer back to the number-one driver of high performance. If you use grades to evaluate an individual, select the desired range that matches the challenges of the job. Yet, even for highly technical jobs, a 4.0 candidate may not have the overall skills to be a great leader, and the candidate with a 2.5 GPA may have hidden leadership abilities that don't show up on a transcript.

Performance management systems that leverage employees' and leaders' innate strengths outperform their peers. It is also why the identification of innate characteristics should drive your high-performing leaders and talent pipeline.

Quantitative Measures

High-performing leaders are always striving to be better, do better, and lead better. It is critical to continue to invest in your leadership team's development and to recognize and reward their progress. On the right side of the dashboard are results measures. There should be four distinct categories:

Progress and Results
1. Leadership impact
2. Department or project impact
3. Company impact
4. Community impact

The leadership impact should be determined by a standardized survey of team members, peers, and leaders that looks for an individual's direct impact on their people, culture, and brand. Currently, one of the most utilized is the Gallup Engagement Survey. This is a 12-question survey that is provided to teams to rate their leaders and company on the drivers of employee engagement. The higher the employee engagement, the higher the productivity and wellness of the individuals. The survey measures how passionate employees are about their jobs, their commitment to the organization, and the amount of discretionary effort they put into their work – the emotional attachment an employee feels about their workplace, leaders, peers, and culture. Leaders are rated against a key set of criteria. Their rating can be compared to those of other leaders in the same industry, thus comparing their leadership effectiveness through team engagement. The best leaders can be found in the top 25% of the band.

Department or project impact. Whether you are a leader or individual contributor, you are responsible for designing and creating results, either by project, responsibility, or department, or a combination of all three if you are an executive. Achieving the goals that were identified at the beginning of the project is your measure of success and should be part of a larger alignment to corporate goals and initiatives for maximum impact. Progress toward the goal may also be considered success, particularly if there are influences outside of the leader's control. Corporate goals could include but are not limited to growth, revenue, or profitability; client loyalty and retention; operational efficiency; and workplace goals for employees, such as engagement.

Company impact. These projects or assignments align directly with a company-wide goal, thus increasing their impact. Feeder projects that align with or supplement main projects are also impactful, creating a foundation for even greater success.

Goals for each project, initiative, or department should be identified at the beginning of the performance year and aligned to specific target dates. A good company-wide measure is the Net Promoter Score, a measure of the loyalty of a company's clients. The tenets of this system should permeate every aspect of your organization, including priority projects and key initiatives.

This is also a good time to address projects that go awry. If projects veer off-course, leaders are not always penalized; rather, the leaders should evaluate the root causes of the issue at hand, whether it could have been prevented and, if so, what was broken. At some point in your career, something will go wrong outside of your immediate control. It's how you handle the recovery that will determine your success. Great leaders know that not everything goes as planned and how you recover can help you not only learn and apply the lesson the next time, but at times is a significant growth opportunity for the individual. Companies and great leaders know this as well.

Community impact. Studies have shown that individuals who have an innate nature of giving (vs. taking) are your better leaders. Those who parlay this into their community effectively are happier, have higher empathy, and provide their resources to others who may not typically have the financial means to engage with someone of this caliber or talent. Nonprofits are especially appreciative of these individuals, and great companies provide a vehicle to easily support your local community. When your highest performers are bettering your community, everyone wins, and your company and brand become stronger because of it.

★★★★★

Credibility weighting or specific algorithms should be created for your specific company and at times for specific roles, but should always be transparent to give each team member and leader the best chance of success. Using a personal leadership dashboard based on the template shown later in this chapter will help your team confront the complexity of evaluating your talent and increase your chances of promoting the right people at the right time.

A great question I've addressed in the past is what if the left side of the equation does not match the right side? That is a good question and begs further analysis to determine why. If the individual is early in their career, they will probably lack high-impact results on the right side of the dashboard. What you are looking for here are indicators of progress of impact over time based upon their level. Are they leading their teams to make an impact? Are they going above and beyond? Are they coaching others toward high performance? Always remember that the left side is the most important and that you, as the leader of the company, are responsible to help an individual make an impact on the right side.

Most often, this is where HR evaluates and determines whether the gap can be closed through experience, learning and application, or more formal training or education. This is where the "development" component of the performance management system will provide candid feedback to the individual, holding them accountable for learning and leveraging the information toward making progress. HR uses the information to identify which programs and projects provide the opportunity, through hands-on experience, to close the gap and move to strength, when possible. A side note worth mentioning here: if an individual does not have a strong base of the number-one most important trait in a leader, their innate personality traits of character, no amount of training will change that. Never allow anyone with a lack of character to penetrate your leadership ranks.

Personal Leadership Dashboard Template

Now it's time to populate the individual dashboard with your new, high-performing criteria using qualitative and quantitative measures:

Drivers	Outcomes
Innate personality traits – including ethics, integrity, grit, trustworthiness	Leadership impact – Gallup Engagement Survey plus employee survey of top 20 leaders
Leadership – GREATNESS to start	Department and project impact – achievement of progress or goals
Intellect – grades are the most accurate predictor of success	Company impact – Net Promoter Score
	Community impact – Community Engagement Score

14

Focus on a Five-Year Plan

Now that you have identified your new high-performing leaders and potentials, developing and retaining them becomes your number-one priority. Setting up a compelling plan for the future is your best hope for creating an atmosphere in which they can thrive will make or break your ability to retain top talent.

While there is a lot to plan as you make this shift to a longer-term high-performance focus, here are three starting points to keeping your most promising leaders challenged, inspired, and motivated:

1. **Compensation and benefits rewards for your high-performing leaders are a must.** Although most leaders are not driven by monetary success, they do expect to be rewarded for their accomplishments and great leadership. Compensate them on the high end of the industry band, particularly if they are ranked in the top 25% of your Gallup

industry indices. Be proactive in your recognition. A high performer should not have to ask for more money.

2. **Provide them with challenging assignments and leadership roles.** High performers have an uncanny ability to figure things out, to think differently, and to inspire their teams to think differently. Leverage this talent by rotating them around your company into roles that both challenge them and are required for your company to remain competitive in the marketplace. Any rotation should be thoughtful, discussed with the individual, and have goals established up front. There should always be a sponsor assigned to them to ensure that they have everything they need to be successful.

3. **Remove their barriers.** Unfortunately, as you transition, some of your lower-performing, imposter leaders and individual contributors will slip through the cracks. Protect your high performers with all you have in your HR arsenal. Keep in mind that high performers are the target of these toxic individuals, and that is the number-one reason they leave organizations. Treat high performers as your most valuable asset. Their sponsor should be able to help them navigate the organization and remove any barriers or people who are hindering their performance. There should be mandatory reporting requirements to the head of HR through the ACT program for any issues. This extra protection will also send a clear signal to the organization that you are serious about the transformation.

To retain high performers, companies should put procedures in place to protect them, including a fast pass to HR and mandatory reporting for leaders and sponsors. HR should have the power to protect the new infrastructure and rules and overrule any internal manager, regardless of their level. This is critical to ensuring a consistently applied high-performance system. In a high-performing organization, the performance review process would play out very differently than in the past. The following is an example of how a high-performing company can promote top employees by merging qualitative and quantitative measurements.

Val was excited to play a role in the promotion process. She had been promoted six months earlier after years of being "on the list." For years she had worked for several bosses who lacked appreciation for her ability to effectively lead her teams, drive some of the firm's highest-priority projects to the finish line, and become an advocate within her industry as a speaker on the conference circuit, presenting the thought leadership she had developed. The organization had finally adopted a new system to identify their talent and, remarkably, she was on the new leadership list! After years of being hidden behind bad bosses, the new system finally identified her as a great leader and placed her in the talent pipeline.

After her promotion, she was aligned to Chuck. Chuck was an incredible leader himself. He held weekly one-on-ones with his direct reports, held skip-levels each year with their direct reports (and each individual in the department), inspired each leader to bring their strengths to their role each and every day, and constantly advocated for larger and better projects so his reports could make a larger impact on the organization. He believed in the new system and leveraged it to help him develop his leaders and team members. He believe that if you developed your people, invested in their progress, and provided valuable and candid feedback, the organization won, and so did the team. He never took the credit for team successes, constantly diverting it to the people doing the work. Yes, he was the leader, but he was confident in himself and in his abilities, never needing to toot his own horn or take the spotlight from others. The new system helped ensure that he never needed to.

Val was armed with each individual's dashboard on her team, and she felt very prepared to fairly represent them at the promotion table, if asked. As a team, they had clearly articulated expectations of what the company expected at each level. In fact, she was going to advocate for two individuals on her team, Jess and Jacob, for two open positions in another department. Although she would feel horrible losing them in her department, that was her job as a leader: to cultivate talent so they could continue to learn and grow. Sometimes that meant moving to a different project or role to expand their impact and abilities. Talented employees within their organization were considered a company resource, not an individual manager's resource, so she was typically entrusted with their care and development for two to three years. With this new system, managers or executives received a rotation of an individual into their department and part of their measurement was to help this person succeed. If they failed, it reflected on both the individual and the leader. As a great leader, no one on Val's team or those rotated off her team to bigger roles was going to fail, and that included Jess and Jacob. They were both up-and-coming talent who were showing signs of becoming high-performing leaders. Both had great qualitative characteristics and quantitative results over time. Both had consistently shown their commitment to learning and progress.

As Val entered the room, the head of HR, Vanessa, welcomed her to the table. She was excited to have the conversation and to share the strategic direction and goals for the coming year. The board had approved her recommendations and she was prepared to execute them throughout the organization.

Vanessa kicked off the meeting by sharing that the board had approved her strategic plan. Over the next five years, the company would become gender-balanced, when possible, including the board and C-suite. This included requiring half female and half male candidates for each posted position, both internally and externally (when interviewing), and the use of new qualitative and quantitative testing for all leadership positions. New roles would be identified and approved by business line management, but HR would identify the talent for those positions, including promotions based upon the dashboard system. Leaders may or may not be involved in the process, but would be notified if one of their team members was selected. All promotions would include discussions with the individual, and the dashboard would include a confidential rotation and development plan for each team member in the company. The data would be placed into a database and individuals would be selected by the new algorithm and thorough discussion and oversight of the HR team, reducing subjectivity and using data and analytics to drive key personnel decisions. This would also ensure consistency of execution across the organization, increasing the probability of success.

Val was excited for this new strategy. It would help the company continue to progress and keep everyone focused on collaborating to find the best solutions for their clients, create efficiencies, and continue to learn and grow. Rotations would ensure that it was no longer about loyalty to one individual, but rather loyalty to the organization, and their clients and people. She was confident the company would now find the best leaders to lead their teams. The company was already starting to see bottom-line results and she could not be more excited for the future.

Both Jess and Jacob were promoted to new roles outside of her department and Val received two new up-and-coming high performers to develop and guide in her department. She was excited for the future and so were they. Armed with the guidance from HR on specifically what they needed to gain exposure to and the innate talents they could leverage in her department, Val used their personal dashboards to establish their performance plan for the year. It was her job to guide and coach them, remove barriers for them, and stretch their strategic thinking by providing insight into the next two levels above them. This hands-on support would prove invaluable to their ongoing development.

Val was engaged and ready to take on the high goals the C-suite had set for her this coming year.

★★★★★

If you are an executive leader, and you are saying to yourself right now, "My company doesn't have this problem and is ready to move ahead like Val's company," the vast majority of you are wrong. If you were to ask women and high performers if they have experienced any of these low-performing inequities in the workplace, the answer from at least 75% of them would be "Yes." This perfectly reveals the dichotomy of the workplace and the reason why progress has not been made.

If you are a board member, C-suite executive, or HR leader in any organization, it is imperative to transform your workplaces into high-performing cultures that promote individuals – both male and female – who exhibit high-performing leadership.

Boards and the C-suite, your leadership is needed now more than ever and will be required through this transformation.

If you don't provide this leadership, this next generation of high-performing talent will do it for you the hard way by seeking out high-performing companies among your competition or waging lawsuits against abusive leaders, costing you millions in brand equity and setting your organization on a slippery slope.

Proactivity is key and can be easier than you think.

Selecting the Right Strategy and Plan for Your Organization

Starting with the right strategy for implementing change will be critical to successful execution throughout your organization. Boards and the C-suite should consider three basic options:

1. **Immediate:** Remove and replace low-performing or abusive leaders legally at all levels. This is the most expensive and disruptive approach.
2. **Short-term:** Identify and give your high-performing and best leaders more scope – they'll set the expectations and hold people accountable. This is your least expensive option, with minimal disruption. It also will give you the best chance of success.
3. **Longer-term:** Remove and replace low-performing or abusive leaders over time. This will be your least effective option

and will most likely fail, as the worst leaders quickly adjust and play the new game. If this method is used, boards need to conduct their own surveys and results to ensure progress. You can use the following chart of the fundamental changes you will need to address during your shift as a guide throughout this process:

Remove the Low-Performing System	Replace with This High-Performing System
Promotions are based upon potential and political savvy.	Promotions are based upon high-performance character + leadership + results over time.
Lead by bullying and abuse at all levels.	Lead by respect and create highly engaged teams at all levels.
Executive positions are held by poor leaders who have their own interests in mind.	Executive positions are earned by the highest-performing leaders who balance the needs of their shareholders, customers, company, and teams.
Performance reviews and compensation are given to favorites and others ad hoc.	Performance review ratings and compensation are given to the highest performers first, then middle. Low performers receive training or realignment to a better-fitting role. Leaders who consistently derail others are quickly removed from leadership positions.
Executives, managers, and employees are highly competitive with each other and play a zero-sum game.	Executives, leaders, and human assets work together to achieve the best results for their shareholders, company, and teams. They work together to compete in their industry, not against each other.

Remove the Low-Performing System	Replace with This High-Performing System
Celebrations focus on winning at all costs.	Celebrations focus on the value created for the client, company, team, and then individual contributions.
Political maneuvering and eliminating internal competition is the name of the game and the way to move up.	High performance, including driving results through highly engaged teams, conducting oneself with the highest of ethics and integrity, and partnering with peers, earns promotions.
Experiences higher-than-average turnover.	Experiences low turnover and highly engaged teams.
Is a culture of distrust.	Trust is core to everything and is earned up to the highest levels through the entire organization.
Gender discrimination, bullying, and abuse are rampant and not addressed. There are few, if any, women in the C-suite and a significantly lower percentage of women than men in leadership roles.	Integration of diversity, including gender diversity, is a top priority. There are short-term goals to create a diverse workplace, including in the C-suite, in five years.
Company performance is a series of short sprints and financial results.	Company performance is about progress, engagement, and clients and can yield up to 41% more revenue than non-high-performing teams.

When selecting a strategy for your organization, it is also imperative that any insight or discussion of the changes planned remain strictly confidential and at the executive level. Any leaking becomes grounds for termination. You cannot make a shift to high performance if imposter leaders are tipped off to the changes. They can adapt quickly and adopt the new leadership characteristics, at least during the transformation period. Once they are entrenched in their new positions, all bets are off and they will revert to their natural imposter behavior, slowing your company's progress and fiscal results.

F – Focus on a Five-Year Plan

Once you have your strategy in place, you need to determine a plan with a defined time period. What gets measured gets done, and goals focused on your talent management should be no different than other C-suite goals, for example, profitability, branding, loyalty, and so on.

With your top-tier HR team and CHRO firmly in place, the board should have established the goals – for example, a 50/50 breakdown of men and women in leadership roles in five years. The team should break this goal down by each year; for example:

Year 1: Define your goal and move swiftly. By the end of year 1, you should have expanded your C-suite and executive team to at least 33% female (if you aren't already there). Take a baseline organizational survey that measures your leaders and culture. The Gallup Engagement Survey is a good starting point. Results should only be shared with the board and C-suite, at least initially. Then educate and train your teams on your new, high-performing expectations. Before making decisions on who will assume key leadership roles, take another pulse check survey. The results should be used to help identify your real high-performing leaders so you can aggregate departments under them.

Year 2: Identify, aggressively promote, and support high-performing leaders based on the new standards. Hiring class and promotions should be as close to 50/50 male and female as possible. Leaders should be hired on new high-performance standards and be trained as teams. These teams should receive frequent leadership training together and alongside existing leaders. You should see fairly immediate positive results.

Year 3: Checkpoint. What is your progress toward achieving your goal? What are the barriers? Year 3 is when it all becomes real. Watch for regression from some leaders in key positions back to the old culture as they feel competition rise and become less competent in the new expectations. Be aggressive when coaching or removing them from leadership roles. Retrain the organization and share progress. By this point, the C-suite should be close to half men, half women.

Year 4: Your bottom line and employee engagement and leadership scores should be showing considerable improvement. Financial goals should also begin to trend upwards.

Year 5: Goal achieved, including a 50/50 gender balance on the board and C-suite. Communicate. Celebrate. Share with your clients. You are leading your industry toward the new standard of a high-performance organization. Like any company goal, you will need to report on progress. This not only keeps the leadership team in check to the board, but it also continually reminds employees of what is most important in your organization to achieve the established goals. Celebrating is one thing most organizations skate past, but it is a powerful way to reinforce and encourage continued momentum.

15

Track and Communicate Your Success

"Don't ever, ever ring the bell."

— Admiral McRaven

What gets measured will get done, but it's also true that what gets celebrated will be replicated. There is work waiting for companies who hope to make the shift to high performance. Those who persevere for years to come will be able to articulate their goals, track them, and then celebrate their accomplishments. Teams thrive when each member's role is recognized and appreciated. Annual goals will keep everyone focused on the goals at hand, create accountability, and provide the opportunity for wins along the way. Yet, in the midst of challenging weeks, don't forget to share both your plan and progress with your teams, particularly at each stage in the process.

This will be your most rewarding time in the company's transformation: experiencing success. To keep your momentum going, recognition and shout-outs will create continued momentum. Teams should be recognized by the executive team in all communications. Remember to also promote your newfound success externally, by submitting for industry awards and releasing your successes in the press. Success breeds success, so celebrate in all ways at all times.

Returning again and again to the five-step SHIFT process will ensure progress and measure what matters – the success of your people and organization:

S – Start with balance at the top. Balance will ensure that your new high-performing expectations permeate the organization.

H – HR's role in the new high-performing company will lead the way, addressing any performance issues immediately, ensuring consistency in selecting new, high performers and holding your leaders to the highest standards.

I – Identifying your high performers and potentials using qualitative and quantitative, technology-driven methods will decrease subjectivity and increase objectivity, promoting the right leaders a majority of the time.

F – Focus on a five-year plan. What gets measured gets done and as a board, C-suite, and company, you will be able to identify your progress toward the annual goal.

T – Track and communicate your success at each step of the way. This will allow you and your company to celebrate your success, reinforce your expectations, gain credibility as a leadership team, and signal to other companies your commitment to high performance.

★★★★★

At the beginning of this book, I promised to share my key lessons after thoughtful prayer and consideration. Regardless of your situation, I hope this helps you put things in perspective:

I learned that bad things happen to good people, especially high performers and women in the workplace, even when you are doing everything right. I also learned that your reaction is your choice and you can make a bad situation a learning opportunity, use it to help other people, or both. I would have never chosen for my job to be eliminated, but if it hadn't happened, I never would have had the opportunity to mentor from a whole new perspective or become truly engaged in our daughter's life at a pivotal moment or spend more time with our son before he left to serve our country in the military. I certainly would not have had the time to make the connection between old-world leadership and the new, inspiring leadership needed for companies to be competitive in the future. I also wouldn't have landed at a company that is committed to progress in our high-performing workplace or supportive of getting this message to the masses.

My job was eliminated on a Friday afternoon, and after a week-end of confusion, I leaned on my faith. I prayed – a lot – and asked why I was in this place. On Monday, after a pivotal conversation with a friend, I woke up and said to myself, "This is going to be the best thing that ever happened to me." I got involved in the com-munity and in my industry. I met people and grew as a person and leader. I was grateful for every moment, every day. To be honest, it was hard some days, and I would revert back to questioning why all of this was happening. I realized that being in great physical shape, rather than candy and chips, made me happier, and I started to get into the best shape of my life. I was able to invest time in relation-ships that had been pushed aside because I was always working. My husband, who was always my best friend and confidant, supported me in taking extra time off to enjoy this newfound freedom and life, which also allowed me to focus on writing this book. In the end, I learned that sometimes it takes your greatest loss to propel you into the shift where you find your greatest joy, or even purpose.

Now I know that my professional "setback" sent me off on one of my most important assignments. It's to share what I know to help other people, which is what great leadership is all about. Ironically, that's all I've ever wanted – to be a great leader who inspires people to achieve more than they ever thought possible, to protect them, and to allow them to shine. And now, I wish the same for you.

Make the Shift

The marketplace has changed and the workplace has failed to follow suit, leaving your organization primed for unnecessary peril and risk. The old, antiquated ways of managing and leading no longer have value or purpose in today's workplace. Instead, leading companies of the future will design workplaces that leverage their greatest asset: their people. These high-performing companies will return HR to the coveted role of leader and champion of the people. They will sit as a valued member in the C-suite and set the infrastructure, norms, and rules of engagement. They will have a direct line to the board and the CEO and will ensure that every leader in your organization is held to the highest standard. If anyone uses derailing, bullying, or abusive tactics, HR will manage the process to help both the leader and the targeted individual. If the leader cannot adapt, they will be fired or moved into a role where they cannot impose their selfish, derailing impact on other people.

With this change, your people will become more engaged, more loyal, and more creative. You may see your shareholder value and productivity increase (all else being equal) and enjoy sustainable progress over time. There will be a renewed sense of team – and family, where everyone has a role and contributes based upon their greatest talents. Leadership roles will once again become coveted positions, not of power, but of positive impact, with the most respected, highly capable performers leading your organization.

To those of us in the C-suite, and who sit on boards and HR, we are responsible to make this shift happen. Are you ready?

Let's do this.

Appendix: Resources

Taking Legal Action

Individuals who encounter bullying or abuse in the workplace should consider reaching out to a top lawyer who specializes in employment law. At a minimum, it is important to gain insight into the law and the best approach to handling the situation moving forward. If there is a legal basis for a case, the lawyer will provide direction and explain the pros and cons and risks.

Laws differ in each state, so researching specific state laws can be a helpful start.

Reporting to the EEOC

When speaking to an attorney, it is important to ask if reporting the situation to the Equal Employment Opportunity Commission (EEOC) is the right approach. Carefully weigh the pros and cons. If the EEOC is engaged and they approve the case, they will act on the individual's behalf to obtain a remedy. Before the EEOC will engage, the individual must first prove that their employer or CEO was made aware of the harassment.

Individuals also need to keep in mind that although it is claimed that the filing will remain anonymous, the EEOC cannot guarantee anonymity. Companies are also kept anonymous, so trying to out the employer through the EEOC is not a fruitful approach. Individuals should consider all options before reporting or engaging with the EEOC.

Nonprofit Support

There are new up-and-coming nonprofits and companies that are designed to help women progress in the workplace. On January 1, 2018, the National Center for Women launched the TIME'S UP Legal Defense Fund. This initiative helps women combat workplace sexual abuse and retaliation by helping to pay their legal fees and connect women with a media platform to tell their stories.

Websites

There also are a host of invaluable resources for women in the workplace. The following are a few website links to help women narrow the search for help.

All Voices
https://www.allvoices.co
> "AllVoices . . . providing a completely safe, anonymous way for people to report issues directly to company leaders. This allows company leadership real transparency into what's happening in their companies – and the motivation to address issues quickly."

Bravely
https://workbravely.com/
> "Bravely connects employees to on-demand professional coaching in the key moments that define the employee experience."

Elected Officials

https://www.usa.gov/elected-officials

Contact your elected officials regarding laws that govern workplaces.

Equal Employment Opportunity Commission

https://www.eeoc.gov/employers/small-business/harassment

Harassment information for small businesses.

Fair Employment Practices Agencies

https://www.eeoc.gov/fair-employment-practices-agencies-fepas-and-dual-filing

"Many states, counties, cities, and towns have their own laws prohibiting discrimination, as well as agencies responsible for enforcing those laws. We call these state and local agencies 'Fair Employment Practices Agencies' (FEPAs). Usually the laws enforced by these agencies are similar to those enforced by EEOC. In some cases, these agencies enforce laws that offer greater protection to workers, such as protection from discrimination because you are married or unmarried, have children or because of your sexual orientation."

Safety @ Work

https://onmogul.com/safety_at_work

"Safety @ Work is a tool that enables you to safely and anonymously report misconduct in the workplace, which are automatedly sent to multiple stakeholders within your organization."

Society for Human Resource Management

https://www.shrm.org/resourcesandtools/tools-and-samples/policies/pages/cms_000554.aspx

Tools for developing policies and procedures for sexual harassment reporting.

StopIt

https://stopitsolutions.com/

"STOPit's frictionless reporting platform combines real-time reporting and real-time messaging, enabling real-time awareness for your organization. The STOPit mobile app is a simple, fast and powerful tool which empowers individuals to protect themselves, others and the organization. STOPit Admin, a robust incident management system, empowers administrators and management to get in front of issues to mitigate risk and adhere to the ever evolving compliance landscape."

Bibliography

Adkins, Amy, "Only 35% of US Managers Are Engaged in Their Jobs," *Gallup*, April 2, 2015a, https://www.gallup.com/work place/236552/managers-engaged-jobs.aspx.

———. "Report: What Separates Great Managers From the Rest," *Gallup*, May 12, 2015b, https://www.gallup.com/work place/236594/report-separates-great-managers-rest.aspx.

Agarwal Dr., Pragya, "Here Is Why We Need to Talk about Bullying in the Workplace," *Forbes*, July 29, 2018, https://www.forbes .com/sites/pragyaagarwaleurope/2018/07/29/workplace-bullying-here-is-why-we-need-to-talk-about-bullying-in-the-work-place/#5248569d3259.

Barnett, Megan, "IBM's Ginni Rometty: Growth and Comfort Do Not Coexist," *Fortune*, October 5, 2011, https://fortune.com/2011/10/05/ibms-ginni-rometty-growth-and-comfort-do-not-coexist/.

Beck, Randall, and Jim Harter, "Managers Account for 70% of Employee Variance," *Gallup*, April 21, 2015, https://news .gallup.com/businessjournal/182792/managers-account-variance-employee-engagement.aspx.

Brooke, Chad, "Toxic Leaders Offer Short-Term Benefits, But Long-Term Problems," *Business News Daily*, June 18, 2017, https://www.businessnewsdaily.com/10014-toxic-leaders-problems.html.

CMOE, "Why Toxic Leaders Will Ruin a Workplace," https://cmoe.com/blog/why-toxic-leaders-will-ruin-a-workplace/. Accessed September 25, 2019.

Crabtree, Steve. "What Information Do Business Leaders Need to Bolster Growth? *Gallup*, February 10, 2020, https://news.gallup.com/opinion/gallup/285650/information-business-leaders-need-bolster-growth.aspx.

Dizikes, Peter, "Workplace Diversity Can Help the Bottom Line," October 7, 2014, *MIT NEWS*, http://news.mit.edu/2014/workplace-diversity-can-help-bottom-line-1007.

Feijó, Fernando R., Débora D. Gräf, Neil Pearce, and Anaclaudia G. Fassa, "Risk Factors for Workplace Bullying: A Systematic Review," *International Journal of Environmental Research and Public Health*, June 16, 2019, https://www.ncbi.nlm.nih.gov/pmc/articles/PMC6603960/.

Workplace Gender Equality Agency, "The Business Case," Australian Government, https://www.wgea.gov.au/topics/workplace-gender-equality/the-business-case. Accessed February 20, 2020.

Huang, Jess, Alexis Krivkovich, Irina Starikova, Lareina Yee, and Delia Zanoschi, "Women in the Workplace 2019," *McKinsey & Company*, October 15, 2019, https://www.mckinsey.com/featured-insights/gender-equality/women-in-the-workplace-2019.

Hyacinth, Brigette, "Employees Don't Leave Companies, They Leave Managers," *LinkedIn*, December 27, 2017, https://www.linkedin.com/pulse/employees-dont-leave-companies-managers-brigette-hyacinth.

Jingcong, Zhao, "New Research: Men Promote Men and Women Promote Women," *PayScale*, May 3, 2018, https://www.payscale.com/career-news/2018/05/new-research-promotion-gap.

Korn/Ferry International, "The Cost of Employee Turnover Due to Failed Diversity Initiatives in the Workplace: The Corporate

Leavers Survey 2007," https://www.kornferry.com/content/dam/kornferry/docs/article-migration/The%20Corporate %20Leavers%20Survey%20.pdf.

Krivkovich, Alexis, Marie-Claude Nadeau, Kelsey Robinson, Nicole Robinson, Irina Starikova, and Lareina Yee, "Women in the Workplace 2018," *McKinsey & Company,* October 23, 2018, https://www.mckinsey.com/featured-insights/gender-equality/women-in-the-workplace-2018.

Kummerow, Kiersten, "Workplace Bullying, Perceived Job Stressors, and Psychological Distress: Gender and Race Differences in the Stress Process," *Social Science Research*, July 2017, https://www.sciencedirect.com/science/article/abs/pii/S004 9089X16305087.

Lam, Bouree, "Why Women Shouldn't Have to Act Like Dudes at Work," *The Atlantic*, July 27, 2015, https://www.theatlantic .com/business/archive/2015/07/women-work-gender-equality-workplace/399503/.

Landel, Michael, "Gender Balance and the Link to Performance," *McKinsey & Company*, February 1, 2015, https://www .mckinsey.com/featured-insights/leadership/gender-balance-and-the-link-to-performance.

Mendelberg, Tali, Christopher F. Karpowitz, and J. Baxter Oliphant, "Gender Inequality in Deliberation: Unpacking the Black Box of Interaction," *Princeton University*, February 7, 2012, https://scholar.princeton.edu/sites/default/files/talim/files/ Gender%20Inequality%20in%20Deliberation%20-%20PDF .pdf.

"Narcissistic Personality Disorder," Mayo Clinic, https://www .mayoclinic.org/diseases-conditions/narcissistic-personality-disorder/symptoms-causes/syc-20366662. Accessed May 28, 2020.

Namie, Dr. Gary, "2017 WBI U.S. Workplace Bullying Survey," *Workplace Bullying Institute,* June 2017, https://www.workplace bullying.org/wbiresearch/wbi-2017-survey/.

Napolitano, Janet, "Women Earn More College Degrees and Men Still Earn More Money," *Forbes*, September 9, 2014, https://www.forbes.com/sites/janetnapolitano/2018/09/04/women-earn-more-college-degrees-and-men-still-earn-more-money/#2480285339f1.

Newman, Greg, "How Can We Better Identify HiPos Using Network Data?" *Trust Sphere*. April 5, 2017, https://www.trustsphere.com/identify-hipos-using-network-data/.

Partners in Leadership, "31 Quotes from Great Leaders on How to Make Employees Happier at Work," *Inc.*, August 9, 2018, https://www.inc.com/partners-in-leadership/31-quotes-from-great-leaders-to-improve-workplace-satisfaction-for-employees.html.

Reilly, Robin, "5 Ways to Improve Employee Engagement Now," *Gallup*, January 7, 2014, https://www.gallup.com/workplace/231581/five-ways-improve-employee-engagement.aspx.

Shore, Leslie, "Gal Interrupted," *Forbes*, January 3, 2017, https://www.forbes.com/sites/womensmedia/2017/01/03/gal-interrupted-why-men-interrupt-women-and-how-to-avert-this-in-the-workplace/#1323123e17c3.

Silverstein, Michael J., and Kate Sayre, "The Female Economy," *Harvard Business Review*, September 2009, https://hbr.org/2009/09/the-female-economy.

Sorenson, Susan, "Employee Engagement Drives Growth," *Gallup*, June 20, 2013, https://www.gallup.com/workplace/236927/employee-engagement-drives-growth.aspx.

Sorenson, Susan, and Keri Garman, "How to Tackle US Employees' Stagnating Engagement," *Gallup*, June 11, 2013, https://news.gallup.com/businessjournal/162953/tackle-employees-stagnating-engagement.aspx.

Van Edwards, Vanessa, "Gender Differences: 6 Fascinating Differences Between Men and Women," *Science of People*, https://www.scienceofpeople.com/gender-differences/. Accessed June 8, 2020.

Index